SEVENTY YEARS WORTH OF TRAVEL

SNIPPETS FROM A COLOURFUL AND INTERESTING LIFE

PAT BACKLEY

This is a travel memoir.
Any references to historical events, people, and places are used as the author remembers them.

Pat Backley
www.patbackley.com

Paperback ISBN: 978-0-473-59901-0
Kindle ISBN: 978-0-473-61805-6
EPub ISBN: 978-0-473-61804-9

Edited by: Colleen Ward
Cover Design: Formattedbooks.com
Formatted by: Formattedbooks.com

Thank you to my wonderful editor, Colleen Ward. She has been with me on every step of my book journey so far and I hope she will want to continue.

This book is dedicated, as always, to my beloved daughter Lucy.
I am so happy that she has inherited my love of travel and adventure.
I must also give my thanks to all the wonderful people I have met during my seventy years of travel; without you, this book would not have been possible.

CONTENTS

MY CURIOSITY IS AROUSED

This book is a memoir of my travels. Seventy years of adventure and new experiences.

A lifetime.

I began my journey in England.

It's a green and pleasant land full of picture-book villages with thatched cottages, fields, and farms. A bucolic landscape.

Of course, if you ventured to London or one of the other big cities, you'd also find magnificent buildings, palaces, castles, and a history of pomp and circumstance. England is famous for its pageantry and ancient traditions.

It's truly a wonderful country, one that tourists flock to so they can soak up the sights or perhaps, trace their roots and explore their heritage.

For me though, as a little girl, it was never quite enough.

I wanted adventure.

Maybe it was because I was brought up by a mother who dreamt of visiting foreign lands.

When I was small she told me about Petra, the rose red city in the desert, a place she had longed to visit since she was young.

One of my mother's favourite books was *Perfume from Provence.* She had bought the book when she was in her twenties, still full of hopes and dreams. Sadly, when she died at the age of 93 years old, she had never visited either of those places. Her foreign travelling had only extended as far as a trip to visit her best friend in Canada, and a rather disastrous weekend in Paris.

Therefore, the mantle was passed down to me, her eldest child. I eagerly accepted this role.

My father had spent the war years in South Africa, serving with the RAF and doing something with planes. I am being intentionally vague about exactly what he did there because he never really explained, but he was an electronics engineer. My best guess is that he helped to keep planes in the air during World War Two.

You see, my dad was much more interested in telling us about his adventures than about his job.

We heard of palm trees, pineapples, sunshine, and curry.

For a young man from the East End of London, life in the military on another continent must have been such a change.

As a little girl, I was fascinated when my father insisted on putting a dollop of curry powder on the side of his plate, no matter what we were eating. He'd even do it with egg and chips, his favourite meal. He often suggested that I try it too, but as a child, I was never brave enough!

I can hear you muttering now—"What a load of nonsense!" But this was all happening in the 1950s, in sleepy, rural England. There were no takeaways apart from fish and chips, no exotic foodstuffs in the shops, just good, old, simple English cooking.

On a particular exciting Saturday when I was about seven or eight years old, Dad came home bearing a big tin of pineapple jam. He was thrilled; he had not tasted pineapples since leaving Africa some 15 years before. I had never tasted them in my life and was instantly hooked. Even now, if I come across pineapple jam in the supermarket, I do a little happy dance in the aisle remembering that day.

So I guess my longing to travel—to see the world beyond my home—was inspired by both my parents' personalities and dreams. Then, Mum got a wonderful atlas from Reader's Digest. Everything intensified.

The book was quite big and had a shiny blue cover. It quickly became a family treasure.

My siblings and I had to ask for permission to open it and admire the wonderful maps inside.

At the time, Mum also subscribed to Look and Learn, a weekly educational magazine for children. These issues were filed in cardboard folders, also to be looked at carefully and with clean hands. It is so funny to write about this now, when so many young children have access to the world at their fingertips via the Internet. Back in the 50s and 60s, however, ordinary girls like me had to rely on the local library or these family treasure troves of wonder.

My dad loved reading and the library; we would often stroll there together, chatting non-stop during the half-hour walk. Then, each of us would spend hours perusing the shelves.

One day I acquired a poster depicting pharaohs of Egypt—I think it was a free gift from Look and Learn—and I stuck it on my bedroom wall. I dreamt of the day when I would be big enough to explore the world for myself.

Eventually, that day arrived.

THE ISLE OF WIGHT

For those of you who know England well, the Isle of Wight seems an unlikely place to start a travel memoir.

I agree—this little island just off the south coast of England and next door to France is hardly the stuff of dreams. For me though, it was the beginning of my wanderlust, a place that, to a ten-year-old girl from an ordinary home, seemed so exotic. My parents had never been able to afford family holidays, so until this point, my travel experience had been limited to day trips to London or the seaside, or a very memorable week in Great Yarmouth at a church summer camp.

So the Isle of Wight seemed like a wonderful adventure. It meant leaving the mainland and going to an *actual* island!

It was a church youth group summer camp, and we travelled by train.

We were twenty or so excited little girls with four volunteer leaders.

After disembarking from the train, we caught the passenger ferry from Portsmouth to Ryde. I was so excited to cross the English Channel; I had never been on a boat before.

Our one-week holiday passed in a flash. We did so many magnificent things (already recorded for posterity in my published memoir) and I fully realised that there was a huge world out there just waiting for me to explore it.

Sadly it took me another five years to venture further afield.

AN EXCITING TRAIN JOURNEY TO YUGOSLAVIA

When I was fifteen, my world expanded.

It was 1966 and a school trip had been organised for us to go to Yugoslavia.

I knew nothing about the country, other than that it sounded different from anything I had ever known. I remembered from my geography lessons that it was located in Europe, bordered by Austria, Hungary, Romania, Bulgaria, and Greece.

This was enough to stir my romantic notions.

Mum said I could go on the trip if I really wanted. This was much to my surprise, as we had never been able to afford such things before. I can even remember being very envious when all my school friends went on our school's skiing trip.

Apparently, an insurance policy she had taken out when I was born was due to mature, and the payout would be just enough to cover the travel costs along with a little spending money. I already had a Saturday job working in the local corner store, so I was confident I could cover any shortfall.

The sea crossing from Harwich to the Hook of Holland is best to remain undescribed in too much detail. In sum, it was a bunch of rather raucous behaviour from a group of some twenty or so teenagers who had been freed from parental constraints. We were trying, but failing, to deal with the rough and choppy crossing, not to mention the boredom after a while and the sea sickness that ensued.

The long train journey through Europe was wonderful though.

To an impressionable teenager, this journey left memories that are still with me some fifty-five years later.

Surly uniformed guards got on the train and demanded to check our passports as we crossed through each border. I had never owned a passport before and was in constant terror every time they appeared, certain something would be wrong with mine and I would be hauled off to be dumped in some foreign dungeon and never heard of again. Of course, that never happened and the trip went smoothly.

We sped through Holland, Germany, and Austria, sometimes being allowed off the train to buy food. We got strange things like hard black bread or funny spiced sausages, foods none of us had ever seen before. At one stop we were herded into the station restaurant, a huge, cavernous place full of shouting and laughter in a foreign language. Enormous pots of steaming soup, containing heaven knows what, were placed in front of us, together with loaves of the same hard black bread.

It was all so new and different, yet somehow familiar to me after all the books and articles I had devoured. In this moment, my senses of wonder and excitement were sparked and my absolute, passionate love of travel was born.

Once in Yugoslavia, we stayed in a modern hotel in Opatija, on the north western coast. Every day we were taken for educational jaunts; we visited the Plitvice Lakes, Pula, Split, and the island of Krk.

I loved the entire trip and was determined that one day, when I was grown up, I would return and see more of the breathtaking country. Now that I am older, Yugoslavia is no longer. Instead, I get to visit Serbia, Croatia, Slovenia, Montenegro, Bosnia, Herzegovina, and Macedonia.

TUNISIA

Despite my love of travel and that fabulous atlas, my sense of geography has never been great.

I chalk it up to not being particularly inspired by the lessons at school. These lessons taught me about the Great Lakes, the Russian Steppes, and the South Pacific, sure, but never with any great passion, and certainly never seemingly applicable to *my* life. If only my teachers had shown me the world as I longed to see it—a world full of exciting differences, but populated with real people who were more similar than we know.

To me, that is what travel has always been about.

It's about the realisation that however differently we all live, however different our food, customs, clothing, beliefs, and language might be, we are all exactly the same. We are all people who want to lead happy lives and provide our families and those we love with the things necessary to live comfortably. We want our children to get a good education so that they can have the chance to achieve more than we have achieved.

I now realise that is exactly why my parents encouraged me to join the library, to read avidly. It's why they spent money they could ill-afford to get that atlas and the weekly copies of

Look and Learn. I will always be incredibly grateful to them both for instilling in me a sense of adventure and wonder at the marvellous world we live in.

When I was eighteen, my fiancé (yes, I know I was far too young, but we all live and learn by our own big mistakes) won a competition. The prize was a one week holiday for two. You could choose between an all-expenses paid trip to a tourist hotel in Spain or something a little more exotic. I persuaded him to see my point, that Tunisia would be nice instead. He was a little nervous about travelling as far as North Africa, but I assured him we would be fine. After all, it was 1969; lots of people now travelled all over the place. We were not able to speak Arabic, but I told him to focus on the fact that it would be hot and sunny. My parents were worried; they did not really approve of their daughter going on holiday alone with a man, even if they were engaged. Somehow I managed to persuade them too—it was the Swinging Sixties after all and I was almost a married woman!

My excitement mounted as we walked through the airport. Only in my wildest dreams had I ever imagined being somewhere as different as this. My fiancé was trailing a bit behind, clearly rather unsure about this place. It was a place where men wore long dresses and ogled his girlfriend.

We stayed in Hammamet at a lovely hotel right on the beach, one of the only hotels in existence there at that time. It was a tranquil spot and we spent hours sunbathing on the golden sand, interrupted only by handsome little boys begging us to buy their oranges or older men peddling their wares. They brought beautiful woven baskets of every shape and size for sale.

Needless to say, I bought what they both had to offer. I had never eaten so many delicious oranges in my life! I did struggle a bit on the plane home though, trying to balance the huge Ali Baba linen basket on my knees. There were no weight or size restrictions on hand luggage in those days!

During our trip we also visited the ancient medina, where I discovered that I was hopeless at haggling. This is a talent that has continued to elude me all these years; I always would much rather pay a high price, assuming that the person selling the goods has a big family to feed and clothe!

I bought lots of souvenirs, gifts for all my family, and a beautiful orange patterned, full-length djellaba for myself.

I can still remember the scent of the jasmine as we walked in the evening along the dusty road leading to the nearest restaurant.

I was hooked. Travel was my absolute passion.

PARIS

A few months later we honeymooned in Paris.

Flying was still rather expensive back in 1970, but it was our honeymoon, so we splashed out.

We stayed at a little hotel in the Madeleine district and spent a week exploring the city. We walked along the Seine wishing our budget would stretch far enough to do a river cruise—particularly the romantic evening one. We walked miles during that trip, admiring the Eiffel Tower, Notre-Dame Cathedral, and the Montmartre district.

I insisted we try the Metro and pored over the map for hours, working out the best way to see as much as we possibly could during our short stay. Following my research, we took the Metro out to the Place de la Bastille, as I was desperate to see the old prison I had read so much about in one of my favourite books about the life of Marie Antoinette.

Imagine my huge disappointment. After dragging my reluctant new spouse all around the area in search of that building, I was told by an elderly Parisian gentleman whom I had been brave enough to ask (in my appallingly bad French accent): "*Pardonne moi monsieur, ou est la Bastille?*"

At first he pretended not to understand me, obviously secretly appalled that this young English woman had never learnt about the destruction of the famous prison in 1789, in the days of the French Revolution.

Despite this dreadful faux pas, I loved Paris then and have re-visited it many times over the years since.

POMPEII AND MOUNT VESUVIUS

I quickly learnt that for me, the ideal holiday had to include some culture, history, and sightseeing, as well as just lying on a beach and soaking up the sun.

When you have a partner who is more interested in hedonistic delights, that can be a bit tricky. Finding a destination that combines the two requires a bit of research. Fortunately I am rather fond of research!

The next trip seemed the ideal solution.

Two weeks, spent in Sorrento on the Neapolitan Riviera. Plenty of sunbathing for him and hopefully a few side trips for me.

We soon discovered that the part of Sorrento we were staying in lacked beaches. Instead, wooden jetties were erected over the stony outcrops, and locals and tourists alike sunbathed on those.

One day on the jetty, we met another couple, a little older and more sophisticated than us. They invited us to join them the next day on a trip to Amalfi, Positano, and Mount Vesuvius.

I was thrilled. The woman was Italian and had grown up in nearby Naples, so would be an excellent guide. He was American, a model for Marlboro cigarettes. They had met at a nightclub in London.

That day was such an adventure. They rented a sports car (sorry, I can't remember what kind!) and we hurtled around the narrow cliff road, high above the Tyrrhenian Sea. The views were magnificent, but much of the time I had my eyes firmly closed, praying we would make it round the next bend! There were no such things as seatbelts at that time, so it was quite a bumpy ride!

We drove at breakneck speed to Amalfi and Positano. I was desperate to stop and explore both places, but everyone else was in a hurry, wanting to reach our next destination before it got too hot.

Mount Vesuvius towered before us, a spectacular sight. I had never seen a real volcano before, but obviously knew about the time it had erupted, destroying the town of Pompeii in 79AD.

It was 1972 and I was 21 years old.

Apparently we were going to climb it, to reach the crater. By this point in the day it was getting pretty hot; the sun was high in the sky and we were totally unprepared for such a hike. My new Italian friend Carmen produced two silk head scarves from her bag and showed me how to tie one, peasant-style, on my head to protect me a little from the sun's rays. None of us had sensible shoes and the lava from the mountain was like walking on nuggets of coal, sometimes causing you to slip. To combat that, the lovely old Italian gentleman at the cash desk had given us walking sticks!

Once we eventually reached the summit, we were escorted, one by one, around the crater by a guide. It was truly terrifying, one of the scariest things I have ever done. There were no railings, nothing but fresh air between me and the active crater. I was more than happy to be able to cling onto the arm of my rather flirtatious, sixty-something-year-old gentleman guide as we slowly walked around the perimeter of the volcano. He explained to me that the reason they now had to escort people one at a time was because, in recent years, a few tourists had committed suicide by jumping into the active crater.

Once we were all safely back from viewing the red centre of the volcano, our guide fried an egg on the surrounding rocks just to prove how hot the area was. Had I known that it was still one of the world's most dangerous volcanoes and that it had erupted as recently as 1944, I would have been a little less enthusiastic about the adventure!

I daresay since it was established as a National Park in 1995 it is more regulated, but in 1972 it was not too touristy. I only remember one small souvenir shop, in which I bought some postcards and a beautiful ring made from the lava, polished to shine like black diamonds. I still have that ring, and looking at it brings back all the memories of that glorious day.

This is why I love souvenirs, just looking at them years later keeps all the memories alive.

The next day we visited Pompeii. Unfortunately, our new friends Tom and Carmen did not want to go—they had seen it all so many times before—but I was desperate. Reluctantly, my husband agreed to tag along on a conducted tour.

That day, much as I loved wandering the old ruins, admiring the columns and footprints of the ancient old city completely destroyed by the eruption, I was sad. Sad obviously, for the people who had lost their lives and homes, but a bit sad too for myself, as I realised that visiting such places on a conducted tour or in the company of an unenthusiastic partner was not good enough. I hated feeling rushed, not being allowed to linger, to soak up the atmosphere in my own time. I realised then that travelling alone, at my own pace, would be something of a luxury. A luxury I knew I would love to possess.

I enjoyed the rest of that trip so much. The long, hilarious lunch with Carmen's loud, extended Italian family, my first taste of pasta, pizza, and sparkling wine, our visit to a local grocer's shop, where the charming old shopkeeper advised my husband to buy a bottle of Riccadonna rather than the Asti Spumante he had selected, as "*It will ensure you a more romantic night!*"

There were a few disappointments as well.

I persuaded him to go on a boat trip over to the Isle of Capri. I had heard of the island and longed to visit; my mum used to sing the old Gracie Fields song about it and I wanted to see it for myself.

Sadly that trip was doomed. My husband had drunk far too much wine and beer the night before, spending the whole crossing being sick. Then, he refused to leave the harbour when we docked, insisting he would be ill if I made him move an inch! I was not brave enough in those days to stand up for myself, so all I saw of "*the beautiful, beautiful Isle of Capri*" were the cobbled, flower-filled streets leading up the hill from the quayside.

You will notice as you read more of this memoir that shopping has always been a major part of my travels. I love to see what is out there, what exquisite souvenirs I can find on my travels.

I bought soft leather gloves in a little shop off the main square in Sorrento. This shop only sold gloves, nothing else. No handbags, shoes, or wallets, just gloves. I chose a pair of beautiful emerald green leather gloves, measured and fitted by the hand of yet another charming elderly Italian gentleman, who intrigued me by pouring a little talcum powder inside the gloves before he gently put my hands inside them, pulling each separate finger down gently in a rather seductive manner.

By this time my husband, fed up watching such a pantomime, had wandered off to the bar next door to sit outside and nurse a beer. Thus, I was able to enjoy the moment alone.

Italy, I love you.

SPAIN

My first trip to Spain back in 1972 was almost my last. Some friends insisted that we join them for a cheap holiday.

It was one week at an all-inclusive hotel in Majorca. I was not keen. I had heard so many stories, and it just didn't seem like my cup of tea. Literally. Apparently, the place was wonderful if you liked "*tea like Mum makes, full English breakfasts, and fish and chips.*"

Now don't get me wrong, I love all those things. But I love them in England, in the place of their birth, not in another country, a place I want to visit because it is different from home.

Forgive me if I have offended you.

I know that many people love home comforts when they travel. I love *some* things, like a comfortable bed and a nice cup of tea, but I also yearn for the differences, the things that make another country exotic and exciting.

Of course I never ended up seeing the real Majorca, so I am in no position to judge.

It was winter, it rained every day, and we barely left the hotel. My companions preferred to sit in the comfort of the hotel bar, whiling away the hours trying out the local beers.

It was to be many years before I returned to Spain and discovered what a fascinating country it really was.

FIJI

Fiji came next. What a contrast.

How was I to know back in 1976, that Fiji would become such a big part of my story? That it would become my spiritual home?

As you already know, despite my love of travel, geography is not my strong suit. When my husband was offered a two-year contract in the Fiji Islands, I had to get out the trusty atlas. I had been convinced it was in the West Indies, so was amazed to find it, a tiny pinprick in the middle of the South Pacific Ocean.

It was just about the farthest you could get from England, so it would definitely be an adventure.

Landing at Nadi Airport at five in the morning after a long flight was a culture shock. In those days the airport terminals were small, quite different from the large, shiny, super smart buildings that stand today.

You used to step straight from the aircraft onto the tarmac and into the tropical heat. Even that early in the morning, the warmth hit you instantly. Coming from a chilly English autumn, it felt like a dream. It was exactly what I had been hoping for.

A real adventure. I stood there, just soaking it all in.

There were lots of handsome smiling men in white shirts and sulus (wrap-around skirts) that showed off their dark, muscular legs. They were rugby playing legs, I later discovered.

There were beautiful women who smiled shyly as they placed leis around our necks and bade us welcome to their beautiful islands. If it weren't for the mosquitoes chewing away on my feet, I would have thought I had died and gone to heaven. Hopefully there are no mosquitoes in heaven; they have been, and continue to be, a bane of my travels—wherever I venture in the world!

With only a two-year stay, I had no wish to waste my precious time just living the expat lifestyle. Tempting as it may have been to spend endless days lying by a pool, drinking cocktails, and gossiping, I wanted more. I wanted to explore my new home, to meet the locals, to discover how they lived.

I was very lucky that I had the perfect person for this, right on my own doorstep. Her name was Naomi. She was my housekeeper. Naomi was a beautiful Fijian lady just eight years older than I, a wife and mother of two young sons. They all came to live in the flat underneath my house and very quickly became my much-loved second family.

Because of Naomi I was able to experience the real Fiji, not just the palm trees, sun, and sandy beaches.

I learned over the course of my time there that Fijians are some of the friendliest, kindest, and most hospitable people in the world. Even if they have very little, they are always willing to share it. I was constantly invited into my friend's homes to share a cup of Punjas tea or a meal—perhaps a lovo with pork, chicken, dalo, and cassava, or some kokonda, rourou, palusami or seagrapes, coconut bread, or lolo buns. And of course, kava.

Also known as yaqona or grog, this non-alcoholic drink is made from the root of the pepper plant. It is presented with a great ceremony, traditionally served from a tanoa, a large wooden bowl that is beautifully carved from hardwood. More often than not, when you visit people in their own homes in the village, kava is made in a large, thick plastic bowl. But however it is served, the presentation of kava is still a common social custom practiced by both indigenous Fijians and Fijian Indians alike.

I have spoken at length about my time in Fiji in my memoirs "*From There to Here, With An Awful Lot In Between,*" so if you are interested in learning more about this fabulous country, perhaps you would like to read that.

I could speak forever about Fiji, waxing lyrical and never run out of things to say. I was 25 years old when I first lived there and it has left an indelible mark on my soul ever since.

I am incredibly fortunate that I have been able to return there many times over the years and I consider it to be my spiritual home, such is my love for the country and its people. I may well not be able to restrain myself and will probably mention it again at some point in this book, but for now I will merely mention a few extra snippets from my first visit.

The beautiful house we lived in, courtesy of my husband's employer, stood in a small cul-de-sac of similarly large detached houses. It was a two-story house surrounded by beautiful gardens with frangipani, hibiscus, fruit and avocado trees and painted in a rather boring shade of cream. The large kitchen was fitted out with plastic faux wood cupboard fronts, so, wanting to stamp my own personality on the place, I—with permission from the owners of course—repainted them. I chose bright yellow for the kitchen cupboards and assured the rather reluctant young Fijian Indian painter that, despite being plastic, with a bit of sanding, the yellow paint would definitely work. He was rather dismissive of my opinion but did as I asked, and that yellow paint was still sticking beautifully to the cupboards when we left two years later. In the meantime, it brightened up the dull kitchen and my spirits beautifully!

The colour I chose to repaint the outside of the house was less well-received by some. After a year or so of living in the tropics, I was used to the brightness of everything—the glorious sunshine, the beautiful flowers, the colourful outfits worn by all my new Fijian friends. So then, the rather boring cream colour of my house was not so appealing. Instead I opted to paint it in a very fetching shade of tropical pink, which I absolutely loved. However, some of my more conservative friends hated it.

Another activity I took up, with Naomi's help, was weaving voivoi fans and bags.

This is a traditional craft that has been passed down through the generations. She taught me how the leaves from the Pandanus plant were harvested, boiled, and then dried in the sun.

Sitting in the shade, cross-legged on an old woven mat, my soul was at peace as I learnt this ancient skill. Voivoi weaving was a craft that was so important to the traditional and ceremonial lives of my hosts. Beautifully-woven mats, often decorated with brightly-coloured woolen edging, are a huge part of many ceremonies in Fiji: births, birthdays, weddings, and funerals.

Almost 50 years later, I can still remember the joy I felt from being taught how to weave and how Naomi and I proudly showed off all my efforts. I created an assortment of fans (which were very important in such a hot country), table mats, and a rather misshapen—but lovingly-woven—handbag.

I am very sad to learn that some of these voivoi plantations in remote villages are now threatened with destruction due to rising sea levels.

Picture, if you can, the contrast.

A few months before this, I had left a dull grey English autumn. Now, here I was on the other side of the world, in a hot, sunny, and colourful new place full of deserted sandy beaches scattered with chunks of coral. There were palm trees and pineapples. Traditional bures (houses) with thatched roofs and walls woven from bamboo. Big rain. Beautiful smiling people whose skin was darker than mine, but whose hearts, hopes, and dreams were exactly the same.

I was just 25 years old and still naïve in many ways, but I soon realised that, although the world was a big exciting place, ultimately everyone, wherever they lived, had the same dreams. They all just wanted to provide a home, food, education, and better future for everyone they loved.

During that two-year stay in Fiji I experienced so much.

The first night in my new home, I was shocked by all the geckos climbing up the wood panelling in the lounge. I was even more shocked when, a few days later, my house resembled a gecko cemetery after my newly-acquired kitten, Marmalade, decided they were tastier than the cat food I was providing.

Lautoka Market became my new shopping experience. Back in 1976 it was an open building with no roof to protect the stallholders from the elements.

At first I was overwhelmed by the piles of exotic and brightly-coloured fruits and vegetables on offer – *What on earth did one do with dalo and cassava?*

I soon realised that it was much easier to go to the market early in the morning, before the sun was too high and the smells followed suit. As well as the permanent stalls, the market was often packed with casual sellers, mostly village folk who had come into town solely to sell their excess produce. Side by side, Fijians and Indians squatted on the pavement, presiding over heaps of tomatoes, huge green lemons, bananas, pineapples, chilies, and ginger. Watching everyone laughing and gossiping while sitting under large umbrellas to shield themselves from the hot and relentless tropical sun, it was easy to forget that for many families, this was their only source of income. The pitiful amounts raised in one day would scarcely buy a couple of cinema tickets back in England. Conscious of this, I often found myself buying far more than I really needed. A heap of bananas from one person for twenty cents, followed by another heap for twenty five cents from a different seller, just because I wanted to help their families. I soon became very adept at baking banana

loaves, banana muffins, and banana cheesecake! Pineapples were another joy, as soon as I had learnt from Naomi the best way to peel and cut them. These were sold in heaps of three or four, strung together with shiny blue or pink plastic raffia. And don't get me started on the mangoes; Fijian mangos are *so* good. Luckily, we had a big tree full of them in our front garden.

There was a small handicrafts section in the market, and it was here that I bought woven baskets, tablemats, tapa cloth, and wooden carvings. When the odd cruise ship came to town, the road leading down to the wharf would be packed with Fijian ladies sitting on the pavement selling their wares. Luckily, because I was now considered a "local," I would never be expected to pay the same price as these "rich" tourists.

During my stay on the island, I experienced several bad hurricanes, the arrival of the Hare Krishna movement, yoga lessons at a Chinese nightclub (Club 21), and day trips to beautiful remote islands that looked exactly like the ones I'd seen in all the travel brochures. Twice-weekly trips to the little library in Lautoka, where Naomi's nephew worked, were a must. I attended a traditional Fijian wedding where both the bride and groom wore tapa cloth. I got to be a guest at a three day Indian wedding, full of excited children, colourful saris, sweets, and henna tattoos. I helped produce a Red Cross newsletter and cuddled numerous beautiful little babies with coconut-scented bodies. I drove around to Fiji's capital, Suva, on a road (the only road) that stopped being paved half way 'round, meaning the remaining few hours were spent navigating dusty unmade roads bordered on one side by sandy beaches and on the other by jungle. It was an adventure that is no longer possible some 45 years, numerous new hotel complexes, and a lot of tarmac later. The Queens Road to Suva is now an easy journey.

I can confidently say I returned to England a completely different person after my wonderful two-year stay in the Fiji Islands.

LOS ANGELES TO LONDON

Leaving Fiji in 1978 was agony for me.

I had become so attached to my life there, and at that point I could never imagine being able to return. I never thought I'd be able to afford to go back and see my beloved Fijian family. Flying was still very expensive and it was so far away from England.

So, it was with a very heavy heart that I boarded the plane bound for Los Angeles.

I had never been to America before; what a culture shock it was.

After spending the last two years living in the tropics with no television, no fast food outlets, and very little contact with the outside world, I was suddenly thrust into a metropolis, a city heaving with traffic, pollution, and noise. A place where I was almost arrested for jaywalking—for ignoring the "*Walk*" and *"Don't Walk" signs.*

Despite my heartbreak, it took me very little time to adjust. After a day or two, I was enthralled by all the city had to offer.

It sounds silly to say this stuff now that the world has moved on so much since the 1970s. Now we have the internet, mobile phones, and cheap easy flights. Television and Google has made the world seem a much smaller, more accessible place. Back then, to an ordinary girl like me, everything seemed so different.

LA was so flamboyant and foreign. Even the sandwiches from Joey's Deli excited me—rye bread stuffed with thick slices of beef, salads of 27 varieties, and lashings of mayonnaise all carefully secured with a pink cocktail stick!

The huge televisions with their seemingly hundreds of different channels.

The small shops and huge department stores filled with all the western decadence I had missed for the last two years.

My few days in LA were topped off with a trip to Disneyland. The Magic Kingdom was everything I had hoped for, having loved Mickey Mouse since I was a little girl. During the evening Grand Parade down Main Street, I sat on the edge of the pavement with all the children and wept unashamedly when he appeared, dancing and waving before my very eyes.

All too soon the trip was over. I had to board another plane, this time heading back to England. But I was determined; one day I would return to explore more of this fascinating country.

BACK TO MY ENGLISH LIFE... TRAVELLING TO THE STATES

It took me a while to settle back into my old life.

I think any sort of foreign travel changes you. I certainly wasn't the same girl I had been before I went to live on the other side of the world.

Life has a funny way of sorting things out. My husband and I started our own business and became a little more affluent, so more travel was in the cards.

He still preferred beach holidays, so we ventured back to the States and stayed on Singer Island in Florida. It was fun, the beaches were great, the shopping was good, and we met a lovely Canadian couple who invited us to join them for dinner one night. They picked us up at our hotel and drove out to a little place at the end of a wooden pier with huge queues waiting patiently outside. They had booked a table ahead of time, so we went straight in. I was amazed to find the tiny place packed full of smartly-dressed people, with newspaper on the tables instead of table cloths. The only thing on the menu was giant prawns, still in their shells. I soon realised that it was quite acceptable to do exactly what everyone around me was doing: peeling the prawns, dumping the shells on the *tablecloth* whilst laughing, and drinking vast quantities of wine and beer. It was such fun. When we were finished and had settled the rather expensive bill, the waitress just whisked off the table-covering and beckoned the next diners in!

Of course I could not resist a little shopping while in Florida, but funds were low. Therefore, I just indulged in a pale-pink linen tablecloth with a dozen matching napkins from a rather smart department store. Unfortunately, I had been thinking of my Fijian table when I bought them; I had forgotten that my table in England was oblong. It is only now, 43 years later, that I actually own a round table suitable to fit the tablecloth!

RHODES AND THE ISLE OF WIGHT

You may not think that these two destinations necessarily go together, but due to my husband's penchant for the beach, they were both places I visited in my twenties.

Obviously I had been to the Isle of Wight before, when I was a little girl, but to go as an adult, a young married woman, was a different experience.

We stayed outside Ryde in a little hotel run by a very fierce woman. When we checked in she gave us a piece of paper listing the rules, but she needn't have bothered as they were also plastered all over our bedroom:

> *Please be respectful to your fellow guests.*
>
> *Do not flush the toilet after 10:00 pm or before 7:00 am.*
>
> *Do not talk loudly; keep noise to a minimum at all times.*
>
> *Breakfast is at 8:00 am; if you arrive after 8:45 am, we regret the kitchen will be closed.*

> *The main door will be locked at 10:30 pm. In the unlikely event that you will be out later than that, please ask at Reception for a key.*
>
> *If you use the bath* (a shared bathroom was on each landing), *please ensure you clean up after yourself. No other guest will enjoy your grubby water!*
>
> *Please ensure you allow at least half an hour to check out. We are a very busy hotel and only have one receptionist who is sometimes rushed off her feet.*
>
> *ENJOY YOUR STAY WITH US.*

Despite that rather crazy set of rules, we did actually have a good time.

We had taken our car over on the ferry with us, so we drove around the island and I introduced my husband to all the places I had been as a little girl—Carisbrooke Castle, Godshill, Blackgang Chine, and Alum Bay. The cliffs with their multi-coloured sand were much as I remembered them, but thanks to new health and safety regulations, we were no longer allowed to scramble up the cliffs and collect our own sand. Instead, we had to traverse the cliff by sedate chairlift and on reaching the top, could visit the souvenir shop to buy a glass container and fill it with the sand of our choice. Sadly, we could not collect it as we had when I was young, directly from the cliffs. Instead, we had to scoop it from big plastic containers. While it was not quite the same experience, it did seem to be very popular. I was just very happy to still have my exciting memories from some 20 years before. Time is not always an improvement.

We ate delicious crab sandwiches outside a little seaside pub at Seaview, wandered around Sandown, Shanklin, and Cowes, and peered into estate agents' windows in Ryde, wondering whether we should think about purchasing a holiday home.

Driving around the coast, we also became aware of the erosion that had taken place. Wrought-iron gates led to sheer drops over the cliffs, desolation where there had once been beautiful coastal homes with fabulous views.

I have been to the Isle of Wight many times over the last 70 years.

One occasion was specifically to attend the National Town Criers Championship, an event I was also lucky enough to witness the previous year, in Hastings on the southeast coast of England. I had made friends with a guy who was an award-winning town crier as well as a fisherman, so I got front row tickets to such competitions and the occasional lobster delivered to my door at 7am. A win- win situation!

Rhodes has been added here as it fell into the same time bracket in my life.

I had always been very keen to visit Greece, to see the ancient buildings, soak up the history, and indulge in some Greek delicacies. However, again, as my husband preferred a beach holiday, I concurred as usual with his decision.

Rhodes, a Greek island, had glorious weather. The Rodos Palace Hotel was quite new and shiny, and it had the most amazing gardens. Every day during our stay, I would watch as the gardeners patiently watered the huge banks of red geraniums. I love red geraniums, so it merely fuelled my desire to have such splendid specimens myself at home. I have since realised over the years that without a full-time gardener to tend to them, they rarely reach such dizzy heights as the ones I saw then!

I strolled around the old town, a medieval city where the Knights of St. John built their first settlement around the small port. The narrow lanes, towers, and fortifications bustled with tourists. I bought myself two statues, rather nice ones of David and Aphrodite. Sadly I had to part with them a few years later after my divorce—I badly needed some spare cash!

ALMOST GOT TO AFRICA AGAIN!

Since our trip to Tunisia back in 1969, I had hankered after more African travel. I had always wanted to visit Egypt, but knew that would be of little interest to my husband, so I quietly dreamt of pyramids and pharaohs, exotic safaris, and seeing baby elephants and giraffes in their natural habitats.

I was thrilled when one day, he mentioned The Gambia. Apparently it appealed to him, as it had sandy beaches and beautiful women!

I was so excited; it may not have been my first choice for an African destination, but who cared? It would be another adventure.

The Gambia, the smallest country in Africa, looked so exotic, although I didn't much like the sound of all the crocodiles. Tragically the elephant, which was once The Gambia's national emblem, had long ago been hunted to extinction. At the time, the last recorded sighting of one there was in 1913.

In reading all the glossy brochures and guidebooks, it looked as though there was enough to keep us both occupied during our planned two-week stay.

Sadly, the adventure never materialised.

The deposit money, which I had been so excited to use to pay for the trip, was lost. My husband decided we could not take the time off work after all; our business was apparently too busy to leave. I did wonder if perhaps his sudden reticence was due to the realisation that he would have to get injections to protect him from yellow fever and the like. He had always hated needles.

So, South Africa is still on my bucket list!

SINGAPORE

1985… New life, new dreams.

Sadly, my first marriage ended in divorce after 14 years. I was pretty heartbroken. When a friend suggested booking an around-the-world trip, I jumped at the chance, especially when this friend said that perhaps we should pop into Fiji while we were at it!

I took a month's leave from my job and set off on another adventure.

Singapore was my first experience of Asia, and I just loved it. We stayed at the Riverview Hotel, a very smart venue on the banks of the river. At that time, most of the riverside area was a bit neglected. It was no longer the bustling place it had once been, but I rather liked it.

We did all the usual tourist things; I shopped to my heart's content on Orchard Road and in Chinatown. We wandered the streets with our cameras at the ready, snapping away at every interesting thing we saw.

Standing outside the People's Park shopping centre, I spotted a cute little boy standing with an older man, obviously his grandfather. I went over and asked permission to take their photograph and we began chatting. The older man explained that his wife and daughter (mother of Kevin, the cute little boy) were inside shopping, and suggested that we wait to meet them. When the women eventually emerged, they seemed surprised to find him chatting to two white people. The People's Park shopping centre was mostly frequented by locals, Chinese families who appreciated the low prices and bargains. It was exactly my kind of shopping!

The family invited us to join them for lunch and that was my first experience of Singaporean street food. Somehow it seemed so much tastier while enjoying it in the company of locals who actually knew the best things to order.

We had a lovely time. Mr. Hock said he had spent his entire working life at the British naval docks. His wife, daughter, and grandson could only speak Mandarin, but we did a lot of smiling and gesticulating. Obviously we passed the test, as they then invited us back to their home on the outskirts of the city.

We travelled with them on the local bus to their home on Lorong 8, a purpose-built complex of tall apartment buildings. There were many of these complexes scattered on the outskirts of the city.

As we stood on the balcony, Mr. Hock pointed out the land where his family used to own a farm. They had only been in the apartment for a year or so, so obviously the pain of losing their home was still quite raw. To lose your family land—the land that your ancestors had farmed for generations—must be incredibly hard. He explained to me, in a very quiet and calm way, that the government had decided it was better for all their citizens (unless you were very wealthy of course) to live in such complexes near the city. He and his wife, alongside all their neighbours, were growing a few flowers and vegetables in pots on their shared landing. The sight of them made me very sad, thinking of what they had lost.

The next day, Mr. Hock and his sons hired a car and took us out to one of the remaining kampongs to visit their friends. These people also had their land compulsorily purchased and were due to move into a tower block the following week. Until then, they were obviously determined to live life the old way, and they proudly showed us all their crops, chickens, and wooden houses on stilts. When I admired their coconut tree, they instantly shook it, picked up two of the nicest looking coconuts, chopped them in half with their machete, and gave the halves to us to drink. It made me incredibly emotional to realise that because of a government decision, these families and many others would be soon forced into a life far different from the one they obviously loved.

A few days later, Mr. Hock's family took us out of town to a huge new temple complex. I loved seeing all the monks wandering around in their orange robes, smiling gently as they tended to their beautifully-manicured gardens or fed the fat koi fish in the huge water lily ponds. The temple complex was new and very beautiful, and they took great delight telling us about all the marvellous tiles—imported directly from mainland China—and what each one represented.

Towards the end of our visit, Mr. Hock took me to a beautiful tiled wall full of little boxes, almost like mail boxes. He explained that nowadays, unless you were very rich and could afford a nice big house in the city, everyone was being moved into complexes like his. "*But we are lucky, I suppose. At least the government lets us live in boxes now; when we die, they put us in boxes too."*

It turned out that this wall contained the ashes of dead citizens, and that their families were allocated one day a year to come here, remove the box, and remember them.

I realised how lucky I was to be shown the city by local people. Mr. Hock's sons took us to eat at the night markets (the best peanut satay I have ever tasted!) and told me which markets were the best for my shopping needs. They showed me all the old shop houses and told me about the history of the river. They also shared exactly which streets the old red light district had been in; it was a place that was apparently much frequented by travelling sailors!

On our last night, they took us to a local fish restaurant full of locals. There was not a tourist in sight, and we were made to select our own live fish to eat from the overcrowded tank in the foyer. That was a slightly tricky moment; I am not a vegetarian, but seeing my next meal swimming around happily was a bit hard to take. Had it not been for the fact that I knew my hosts would be offended, I would probably have asked for just vegetables!

That aside, we had a wonderful evening. There were about twenty of us in all, the direct family and a few additional cousins and aunties. The fish was delicious and although the men drank the local Tiger beer, I joined Mrs. Hock and the other ladies and only drank the tea that was offered. After about ten small cups of this, Mrs. Hock lifted the lid to show me the chrysanthemum flowers floating on the top. I admitted that it was my first and only time drinking such delicious tea, and one of the aunties explained that it was very good for digestion!

They all came to the airport to bid us farewell the next day, and I was given gifts of a beautiful orchid brooch and a pretty patterned skirt, handmade by one of the family's tailor aunties. We kept in touch for a few years, exchanging Christmas cards and the odd letter. Sadly one day my letter was returned, "*Address Unknown,*" and since this was way before the internet and Facebook, we lost touch. It is so much easier these days; now there is no excuse for not keeping in contact with friends and acquaintances.

LET'S DO ADELAIDE, THEN POP INTO FIJI

Adelaide was fun.

It was 1986 and I was on my first ever trip to Australia, so it was exciting to be met at the airport by a toy koala that played Waltzing Matilda. Vi, Peter, and their grandson, old friends of my travelling companion, were also there to greet us.

They were English—*Ten Pound Poms*—and had taken advantage of the opportunity to move to Australia 20 years earlier to seek a better life. It had been a brave decision; they had no family there, no jobs or home to go to, and they had three young children. Luckily, it had all worked. They were settled in a nice residential area north of the city, Elizabeth North, in a detached brick built house with a large garden, fruit trees, and a swimming pool.

Vi told me how she had been anxious as a young mother, dragging her children across the world to an unknown future. She talked of how her kids and Peter, her husband, had loved the long sea journey, whilst she had hated it and had been endlessly both homesick and seasick. They were ordinary people who left their ordinary lives behind. Peter had lost his job in England and they could never imagine being able to afford their own home there, which they wanted badly.

"And then we arrived here. For the first six weeks, we stayed with all the other immigrants at a hostel on Glenelg Beach. The kids loved it, swam in the sea all day long, and Peter soon found a job. A few months later we got the chance to put down a deposit on this place, and we've been here ever since."

The pride in her voice was unmistakable. They had made a good life for themselves and their children in this far-off foreign land.

I sunbathed in their garden, my drink balanced beside me in a red tulip-shaped metal drink holder. Sadly I never thought to buy one of these clever contraptions for myself to take home, and the memory of it has haunted me for years!

They took us all around the city and showed us the new casino. Then, they took us on a wonderful Murray River cruise, a Barossa Valley wine tasting tour, and a visit to a wildlife centre owned by their friend, where I was allowed to cuddle a real live koala.

We were sad to leave; it had been a marvellous few days!

But it was now time to head to my beloved Fiji.

It had been eight long years since I left the Fiji Islands, a group of 333 islands in the South Pacific. It was a place I had never expected to be able to visit again, a place that was firmly in my heart.

We checked into the Regent Hotel on Denarau beach.

In 1986, this was the only hotel on Denarau Island and it was frequented by film stars and the like. Now, almost 40 years later, the island is unrecognisable, a shiny glitzy place of big hotels, villas, shops, water parks, and a bustling marina.

On my first day in the hotel, I bumped into Christopher Lee. He and his wife were absolutely charming and were obviously enjoying their stay in this rather exclusive hotel, without being chased by the paparazzi.

I thoroughly enjoyed all the luxury of the hotel, of course.

I knew it well. When I lived here in the late 1970s, we visited often.

As locals living in the area, we had always been welcome as day guests. We had also spent one Christmas and New Year holiday in the hotel. Like the kids on the beach, I had been so excited when Father Christmas appeared over the horizon, standing in a speedboat, coming to deliver gifts to us all.

I loved the cool (as in air-conditioned) hotel entrance and the fascinating old photos showing the Fiji of yesteryear. The art depicted fierce looking warriors with their dreadlocks and spears. There was a long impressive glass coffee table full of exotic shells, and calm, friendly, warm, yet highly-efficient service from the staff.

I still remember—with great fondness—eating pineapple and chicken salad, served in half a pineapple skin, whilst the gentle tropical breeze wafted around the open air dining room on the beach. I can remember relaxing in the enormous, stylish bedrooms, where large framed tapa cloth pictures adorned the walls. I strolled along the lengthy sandy beach at sunset, barely meeting another soul except for the one local expat lady who assured me that if I only sunbathed before 9.30am and after 4.30pm, I would never get sunburnt!

I sipped exotic cocktails at the pool bar whilst swimming in the warm turquoise water, and chatted to the hotel gardeners as they watered and pruned the exotic vegetation. There was- the beautifully perfumed frangipanis, the colourful hibiscus, and the birds of paradise.

But of course the most exciting bit of the whole trip, the real reason for my visit, was to see my beloved Naomi and the rest of my Fijian family.

When we left the islands back in 1978, Naomi had decided to give up being a housekeeper and instead, took a job working as a ward maid at Lautoka Hospital. Her uncle had given her a piece of land in Tavakubu Village and Semesa, her husband, along with the men from the village, had worked hard to build a house for them to move into after we left. I saw them doing this, amazed at the enormous lengths of bamboo they had cut down from the forest to weave the walls. I watched fascinated, as Semesa, wearing thick gloves, skilfully wove these into walls for his family's house.

When it was finished a few weeks later, he invited me to the village. I had to fight very hard to hold back my tears that day; the little house had been so lovingly constructed. Semesa had even made Naomi little bookshelves to house her Bible and my old earmarked copies of Time Life magazine. The brightly-coloured curtains she had made hung proudly at the windows and there were new embroidered pillowcases and mats on the table.

"*One day,*" said Semesa, "*I shall build on a kitchen.*"

And when I went back in 1987, he had. He had also added a small lean-to shower and replaced the lovely woven walls with ones of tin. When I asked Naomi why, she replied "*Oh Marama, if my house is just made from stuff from the forest, people will think I am poor."*

It was so wonderful to see them all again. We sat cross-legged on woven mats on the floor of her little house and talked for hours. Various relatives pottered in the background, listening to our conversation whilst preparing tea, cakes, and grog. Of course we had to drink grog, presented as always in the traditional way. I was home.

BACK TO L.A.

In 1987, I returned to Los Angeles.

It was time for another little adventure. I was divorced and had a new boyfriend.

When he suggested a little trip to the States, I needed no persuading. My ticket was purchased that very day.

We flew to LA and hired a car, then drove to San Francisco via Carmel and the coast. It was a truly beautiful drive and I was very keen to visit Carmel, where the actor Clint Eastwood had been mayor for many years. We decided to camp, in the car, in Yosemite National Park. I was rather envious of all the big RVs at the campground with their awnings, portable showers, and real beds. We coped reasonably well in our substandard accommodation, although I was too terrified to leave the car at night in case of bears. It was definitely the right decision; when we got up the next morning there were new scratches on the steel locker, where, as instructed, we had stored all our foodstuffs, even our toothpaste. Apparently, bears have an excellent sense of smell.

Yosemite was beautiful, with vast open spaces and huge majestic redwood trees.

We drove through Death Valley and my boyfriend thought I was crazy because I insisted on getting out of the car to look for interesting rocks. I have always been something of a rock person, collecting them on my travels around the world. This trip was to be no different!

We visited the Hoover Dam—a marvellous feat of engineering—housed in pristine Art Deco style. I must confess to being more interested in the history and architecture than the workings of the dam itself, but it is definitely worth a visit.

We swam in Lake Tahoe and Lake Mead. I scraped my knee on a rock and still have the scar to this day. We drove through old ghost towns and my vivid imagination was sparked, thinking of all the lives that had been lived in those small isolated places.

We stopped one evening in a remote bar, where whilst drinking my cold beer, I turned to smile at the man sitting beside me as he remarked on my "*cute British accent.*" I fear that my jaw dropped, as I came face to face with a Native American. He was a very handsome man in a white shirt and blue jeans, his dark hair tied back in a ponytail. He could easily have come straight out of one of the Cowboy and Indian books my little brother loved so much.

He gave me a knowing smile. "*Yes, I am.*"

Nothing more needed to be said. He knew exactly what I was thinking. My boyfriend and I had a fabulous conversation with him. It turned out he lived locally, and the next day he invited us to a reservation to see how his people lived.

The experience broke my heart. These once-proud warriors, who for centuries had freely walked the land, were now forced to live in small, confined spaces. He explained that alcohol, poverty, and despair were destroying many of his people. It was such a stark contrast to the image projected at tourist sites, where smiling Native Americans sat outside teepees, carving wood or stone.

We went to Las Vegas, a place I had never been particularly interested in visiting. Because we were so close, it seemed silly not to see what it was all about.

Back in 1987, Vegas was not as big and flashy as it is now. However, we still enjoyed wandering the Strip, popping into a couple of casinos to waste bucketfuls of coins on the slot machines. I even suggested to my boyfriend that perhaps we should pop into one of the little wedding chapels and get married while we were there, but he sadly declined my generous offer!

We had not booked any accommodation in Vegas ahead of time, so we ended up paying a lot of money for a rather dubious hotel on the edge of the Strip and spent an uncomfortable night trying to come to grips with the waterbed!

Once in San Francisco, I was desperate to go over to Alcatraz to see the old prison. Sadly there were no tickets available, and I was told I should have booked weeks in advance for such a popular venue!

LET'S TRY SKIING

A few months after our return from the States, my boyfriend suggested we take a skiing trip. He was an excellent skier and, despite my reticence, he assured me I would pick it up in no time.

Now I have never much liked the cold, I hate heights, and have no real desire to balance on silly little planks of wood, fibreglass, or whatever skis are made of these days. But, he persuaded me! And of course, it provided an opportunity for me to buy special clothes.

He took me to a local ski shop where I tried on desperately uncomfortable ski boots. I perked up a bit when I saw all the brightly-coloured ski wear—the anoraks, leggings, and all-in-one snowsuits. He said I was being ridiculous, spending money on such things before I even knew if I liked being on the mountains, and that I would be much better just hiring everything when we got to our destination.

Ignoring such sensible advice, I bought a red, white, and blue snow jacket, padded red trousers, matching gloves, a hat, and goggles. At least I now felt a bit prepared.

A few days later, I also acquired numerous pairs of thermal underwear and a few nice little après ski outfits. At this point, I was finally ready to ski.

We flew to Italy then got a coach to Livorno, our destination. It was evening when we arrived in the pretty little alpine village and I was happy to see that it matched the brochure. Lots of old chalets and a nice little main street with plenty of restaurants and bars to enjoy après ski.

The next morning, reality hit. Having rented my horrible bulky ski boots, I followed my boyfriend across the car park to the ski lift.

"*Don't worry, we're just doing the nursery run this morning. Just so you can learn the ropes.*"

As far as I was concerned, the nursery slope might as well have been the hardest, most difficult black run. I could not control my skis at all, I fell over constantly, and I hated the button lift. I fell off it a couple of times and was mortified to see small children laughing at my discomfort. They would whizz past me down the gentle slope while I was trying, for the umpteenth time, to perfect my snow plough technique.

I promise I tried my best, but I never really improved. I did get dragged up to other, higher slopes and my boyfriend did his best to be patient, but for an experienced skier like him it was probably tortuous trying to remain a calm, loving partner whilst being utterly frustrated at my lack of ability. Still, we survived the week somehow and I have happy memories, mostly of the hot chocolate drinks at the top of the mountain café and all the après ski meals. Particularly, the cheese fondues!

We did go on several more skiing holidays over the years, but I am ashamed to say I never really improved. I think I was too fearful of hurting myself to relax properly!

THE BAHAMAS

"Bermuda sounds nice."

Back in the 1970s, this was a catchphrase from an old television commercial for Imperial Leather soap. But this snippet is not about Bermuda.

I already knew, from my years spent living in Fiji, that tropical islands and I got on very well. When my boyfriend mentioned that he was thinking of applying for a job in the Bahamas, I jumped at the opportunity and suggested that perhaps, we should try it out first by booking a little holiday there.

We flew to Nassau and wandered the streets, visiting the market—where of course, I purchased yet another woven basket and a couple of bright sundresses—and chatted to the locals. We rented a car and drove around a little, admiring all the architecture, the modest homes and the huge, glitzy mansions. We tried the local delicacy—meat from the Conch shell—and drank exotic cocktails in little backstreet bars. We watched all the shiny new hotels and resorts being built and realised that we had come at the right time to see Nassau before it was completely overrun with tourists.

We ventured further afield, out to the island of Eleuthera. One of our friends was the general manager of a beautiful, very exclusive hotel there, so we enjoyed a little tour of the stunning accommodation and the pink sandy beach. The three of us wandered to a quiet cove nearby and our friend told us how they often found packages there, dropped by drug smugglers.

Then we went to the Family Islands, which is where the proposed job offer was. I remember being so excited. If he accepted the job, we would be given a free house to live in, right on the sandy beach. In my head I already knew exactly how I would furnish it, with just the right mix of local and European fabrics and furniture to make it interesting.

Imagine my disappointment then when, after being offered the job, he changed his mind and decided to stay in England. I never got the chance to live in the Bahamas after all.

DEVON AND CORNWALL

Anyone who knows these places will agree with me that they are very special. Located at the very tip of southwest England, Devon and Cornwall have much to offer to the traveller.

Both have long histories, histories of smuggling, uprisings, tin mining, and ancient naval traditions. Old medieval market towns rub shoulders with forests and moors. History abounds in every corner of the region.

There are magnificent sandy beaches, remote coves, wonderful cliff walks, castle ruins, and old fishing villages, many of which have remained virtually unchanged for hundreds of years. Old stone churches and cathedrals, ancient steps, and cobbled streets can all be found here.

Writers and artists have, for centuries, been attracted to such places.

Just driving around the narrow, winding country lanes gives you a sense of the history. Farm gates and kissing stiles remain where they have been for hundreds of years; it is only the humans who change.

I have been lucky enough to visit these fabulous places on and off for the last 50 years and I am never disappointed. There are so many wonderful sights, so many delightful places, far more than I could begin to list here.

Although, since I am tempted, I will mention Dartmoor, Plymouth Hoe—from where Francis Drake sailed to defeat the Spanish Armada back in 1588–Polperro, Newquay (where, at the tender age of seventeen, I bought a rather fetching artist smock, imagining it would improve my painting skills!), Burgh Island, Dartmouth—home of the famous naval college—Salcombe, Totnes, and Land's End. There are cornish pasties and cream teas. This region truly has it all.

EGYPT

At the age of 40, I finally made it to Egypt.

Heartbroken after yet another broken romance, I needed a change of scene. When I spotted an advert for cheap flights, I booked one with barely a second glance.

I travelled alone and am so glad I did; it proved to be one of the most wonderful holidays I have ever had. Whilst it can be a little lonely at times, solo travel has some great advantages. You can do what you want, when you want, without taking anyone else's wishes into consideration. My trip to the place I had fantasised about since I was a little girl proved to be everything I had imagined and more.

I stayed in Luxor, in a modern hotel just a short walk from the old town. It was the perfect place—a haven after a hard day's sightseeing—nestled on the banks of the river Nile with beautifully-manicured, perfumed gardens leading down to the water.

I sailed on the Nile in a felucca, a traditional kind of sailboat. It was just the handsome young boat owner and me. I was thoroughly enjoying this leisurely mode of travel; it was so much nicer than the rather overcrowded tourist boats that passed us as we sailed gracefully along. Then, the owner mentioned the crocodiles… the romantic moment passed. I was rather relieved when he dropped me back at the hotel.

What can I say about the West Bank and the Valley of the Kings?

If, like me, you would rather avoid the hordes of tourists, I'd recommend going very early in the morning—before the sun is too hot and all the tour buses arrive.

I went in February, a little out of season, and it was the perfect time.

Many words and guidebooks have been written about this area, so I will just add my thoughts. Go if you possibly can. Talk to the locals. They will point out the sites that are not in the guidebooks. If you are lucky, they might even show you some real treasures, like the tombs in the Valley of the Nobles. While these are less visited spots than the likes of Tutankhamun, they are just as inspiring.

Having just supported the idea of sightseeing with the locals, after I had followed a couple of very charming Egyptian men down into the bowels of the earth, I did fleetingly wonder how sensible it was. No one knew where I was; perhaps I would never emerge and would spend my last days locked in an ancient tomb.

But of course, all was fine. I saw wonderful wall paintings and really experienced the true Egypt. When we emerged, blinking in the bright sunlight, we were invited into the little village hall to partake in a cup of delicious mint tea. The village children crowded around me and of course, I purchased some of their offered wares: a statue of a sleek Egyptian cat and some scarabeus.

Another day of the trip, while I was wandering alone around Luxor Temple, I met a group of local children on a school outing. I chatted happily to their teachers and posed as requested with all the children. Later that morning, I chatted with one of the temple guides asking him whether the ruins next to us were indeed Roman. He practically spat out his answer; apparently his countrymen despised the Romans for the way they had desecrated the Egyptian treasures, temples, and statues. In exchange, they now used the Roman ruins in Luxor town as a bit of a rubbish tip, discarding their newspapers and drink bottles there. He was amazed when I explained to him that in England, if even a tiny area of Roman ruins or marble floors were discovered, they were covered in glass and protected, and people were then charged to view them.

I could list so many things you must try to see in Egypt, but I will attempt to refrain from sounding like a guidebook. This is supposed to be a travel memoir—something to amuse rather than instruct!

The light show at Karnak Temple is a must.

One must also wander 'round all the shops and bazaars, if only to purchase fine Egyptian cotton sheets and tablecloths.

Queen Hatshepsut's mortuary temple, an amazing edifice in the desert, is another site to see. It's three massive terraces of limestone, sandstone, and granite are a masterpiece of ancient architecture.

A few more things to do during your stay: visit the Abu Simbel Temples and the Colossi of Memnon, and grab a drink at the historic Winter Palace hotel.

Walking back from Luxor town one afternoon, I met a young Egyptian boy called Mohammed, who asked if he could walk alongside me to practice his English. Travelling as a single woman, I had been subject to many such proposals by older men—some offering a little more than a language lesson—but there was something endearing about this boy, so I agreed.

By the time we reached my hotel, I felt so comfortable with him that I agreed to go to his home and meet his family. They lived about a mile out of town in a small village of mud-built houses, and as we approached, a crowd of excited children greeted us. Once in his home, I sat on a bed with his four sisters. None of them spoke a word of English as they ate the pigeon his mother cooked for us while watching a flickering black and white television. His father arrived and was a little surprised to see me sitting there with his daughters, but he was absolutely charming. Only the men in the family could speak English; it was not considered necessary for the girls to go to school for long enough to learn it.

Mohammed and his father walked me back to my hotel that evening, and as I strolled beside the Nile with these two men, both wearing their traditional garb, I thought about how rural Egypt was—almost totally unchanged from biblical days… if you discounted the odd car and telegraph wire!

The next day, Mohammed's family took me to a local camel market, which was fascinating. I was the only woman there. A white woman amongst so many men, yet I never felt anxious. We then went back to the village, as apparently Mohammed's grandma, the matriarch of the family, wanted to meet me.

Introductions over, I had to wait patiently while they all changed into their best clothes so that I could take their photo.

(Remember that this was long before the days of mobile phones capable of shooting good pictures.) I got the photos from my camera processed at the hotel, paying an exorbitant amount for a speedy service, and was able to hand the family several prints before I left Luxor.

I often chatted to some of the young salespeople at a nearby shop and learnt that they were Coptic Christians, which was unusual in a predominantly Muslim country. When I popped in on my last day to say goodbye, one of the young men shyly handed me a gift, a little silver ring he had made for me in the shape of a cross.

I have been very blessed. In all my travels around the world, I have often been gifted small things—things given with love, just because of my passionate interest in ordinary people and their lives.

After leaving Luxor, it was off to Cairo for a whistle-stop tour. I flew there, my limited time in this fascinating country too short to waste precious hours travelling.

I had booked a local driver to meet me at the airport, as I had heard that Cairo traffic was a little frantic.

Ahmed was a very handsome Egyptian man, aged 35. He told me this as we sat over a glass of mint tea in the foyer of the Hilton. My room was not yet ready and he insisted that I, an unmarried woman, should not sit in the hotel alone. Apparently it was his duty to ensure that as an esteemed client, I was delivered to my destination safely. He also explained that although he still lived at home with his parents, he was ready to find a nice wife and settle down. Apparently, he felt that I would be a suitable candidate and assured me that he could have me nicely settled in a little flat in Cairo and pregnant by the end of the year!

I loved my quick trip to Cairo. I visited the pyramids and was able to climb inside one, eventually crawling right down to the burial chamber. It was a rather claustrophobic experience, and so I felt incredibly relieved when I emerged, back into the real world. I admired the Sphinx and adored my morning trip to the then overcrowded and rather muddled Cairo Museum. I marvelled at all of the ancient treasures that filled the space. Everything I had read about as a child in the Look and Learn magazines were now right before my very eyes.

I hired a taxi one evening to take me to the Khan el-Khalili bazaar.

The driver, a wizened old man, was horrified that I intended to visit such a place alone—especially at night—and told me in no uncertain terms that he would be waiting right outside to ensure I got back to the hotel safely.

He needn't have worried; I was perfectly safe. By now I was used to all the advances, the compliments about how I was worth at least ten camels, and how happy I would be if I just bought someone's fabulous carpet.

I wandered around the ancient old souk, admiring the medieval Islamic architecture and soaking up the wonderful atmosphere. Thousands of stained glass lamps, sparkling silverware, and beautiful handmade carpets glowed in the evening light, and the heady smells of exotic perfumes and spices transported you to another world. It was all I had imagined and more. I was offered arm massages, gold jewellery, and several beds for the night. I emerged hours later, laden down with my purchases of tiny glass perfume bottles, beautiful mirrors, exotic jewellery, amber and jasmine scents, and a rather nice t-shirt with a pharaoh's face encrusted in coloured sequins!

True to his promise, my taxi driver was still waiting outside when I was finished, and was obviously relieved to see me emerge in one piece. I went back to the hotel, had a celebratory last drink in the crowded bar, was propositioned by two very attractive Egyptian gentlemen on my way to the lift (whom I politely refused, you will be relieved to hear!), and left Cairo early the next morning. I was sad to be leaving such an exciting place—a place I had been desperate to visit since I was a little girl. However, there was still so much of the world to see.

NORTHUMBERLAND AND SCOTLAND

Although I had lived in England all my life, like many people, I had never really seen much of my own country. It took me 42 years to get across the border to Scotland.

Staying in Northumberland with my new husband's relatives, I realised what a lot I had missed. Northern England is very beautiful, particularly the rural areas.

Having said that, I also found a lot of charm in many of the towns and cities. Newcastle has many splendid buildings and a fine waterfront area that was being regenerated when I was there. Old warehouses were being turned into restaurants, offices, and smart apartments.

Then there is the lovely old market town of Hexham, a most attractive place full of antique shops, tea rooms, and a fine Anglo-Saxon abbey. You can even visit England's first purpose-built prison, the Old Gaol, now restored as a museum that tells of the bloody history of the town, the marauding Vikings, and the Border reivers.

Corbridge is another ancient place. Once a Roman garrison town, it is now better known for its beautiful shops and fine stone houses.

There are plenty of quaint pubs, inns, and bed and breakfasts in which to stay if you fancy a change from the faceless hotel chains.

Beautiful wild sandy beaches, castles, waterfalls, pretty little villages, thriving farms, and wild moorlands. This county has it all.

And of course there is Hadrian's Wall, now a Unesco World Heritage site. It was built in 122AD, a feat of engineering by the Roman Empire. If you are feeling energetic and have several days to spare, you could walk the whole 73 miles of the wall from Newcastle to Carlisle, starting at Wallsend in the east and finishing at Bowness on Solway in the west. I only had one day to spare, so I just walked the last portion, but it was an experience I will never forget.

It is also worth visiting Vindolanda, the site of an ancient fort, a place that generations of Roman soldiers and their families called home. Now it is a thriving tourist attraction, a wonderful place where you can see history come to life before your eyes, quite literally. Here you can watch live archaeological excavations taking place. "*No other Roman site in Britain is as rich in its findings. Everything on display in the museum was found from the Roman site, only yards away.*"

If, after absorbing all that history, you yearn for wide open spaces, you can pop to Kielder Water and Forest Park, a playground for cyclists and walkers, and a haven for wildlife.

Venture a little further north and you will come to the charming town of Jedburgh, on the England/Scotland border. With its connections to Mary, Queen of Scots, this ancient town has much to offer the Abbey, the Mary, Queen of Scots House, and Castle Jail are just a few sites. If you visit between May and July, you may be lucky enough to see the Common Ridings, a recreated spectacle, part of the Callings Festival. Or perhaps you are more interested in visiting Jedforest, one of the world's oldest and most famous rugby union clubs.

Next we hopped to Edinburgh, Scotland's compact, rather hilly capital.

It is a place of so much history, with its medieval Old Town and rather more elegant, Georgian New Town. The entire city is presided over by Edinburgh Castle, home to Scotland's history and crown jewels.

There is so much to see in this city, you must try to allow a few days to absorb it all.

We stayed on the Royal Mile, right in the centre of the city, so it was easy to walk everywhere. We absorbed the sights and sounds as we strolled the ancient cobbled streets. I have mentioned my passion for architecture and this place had it all, everywhere I looked.

We went to the Royal Military Edinburgh Tattoo, held on the castle grounds. It was a dark evening in August and, sitting on temporary scaffolding with some 8,000 other people, I found it incredibly moving. I have always loved military bands, and to witness such a spectacle as this was wonderful. The music, the pomp and ceremony, the colours of all the uniforms, the fireworks. Definitely a night to remember.

From there we drove to Inverness, capital of the Scottish Highlands.

We stopped en route at a lovely old hotel in Nairn, right on the beach. It was a place you could imagine Agatha Christie choosing to stay in to write one of her books. Here we were served delicious fresh scallops and kippers for breakfast.

Isn't it funny, the things you remember? I would be very hard pushed to remember any other meals during that trip, but even now, fifteen years later, I can still taste those scallops!

Inverness is another ancient town full of stone buildings, castles, and history.

We searched Loch Ness, but didn't spot Nessie. We visited Culloden Battlefield, where Bonnie Prince Charlie and his Jacobite army had taken their last stand. We drove over hill and dale, admiring the magnificent scenery as we went. I so wished there had been time to see more. I craved to explore the rest of the Highlands, the outlying islands, Dundee, Perth, Aberdeen, Stirling and Glasgow. There is still so much of Scotland left on my bucket list.

TAKING MY TWO-YEAR-OLD AROUND THE WORLD

In 1996 we were offered a real adventure.

My new husband was offered a teacher exchange, so we agreed to spend a whole year swapping lives with a New Zealand teacher and his family by living in each other's homes.

Lucy, our daughter, was only two, so it seemed like the ideal time to do it.

Although she was quite tiny, she was such an adventurous little girl. We never thought twice about dragging her all around the world, away from everything and everyone she had ever known.

We started our adventure in Bangkok, so that was a pretty exciting place to begin the journey. It was Christmastime, and the bustling city was dressed in its festive best, tinsel, baubles, and sparkly stars as far as the eye could see. We stayed in a lovely hotel right in the city centre, so it was easy to explore everywhere on foot. The first night we were pretty tired—too tired to persuade our little jet-lagged daughter to try some of the local fare—so we opted instead for McDonald's. As we left the restaurant, emerging into the humid early evening rush-hour traffic, Lucy's little voice piped up.

"*Mum, look at that elephant.*"

I looked down at the little purple plastic elephant she was clutching in her hand, her McDonald's Happy Meal gift.

"*No, not this one. Look over there!*"

Much to my amazement, there was a huge elephant weaving through the busy traffic. It was obviously a regular event, as we were the only ones who seemed surprised. What a wonderful introduction to exotic foreign travel for my little English country village-born daughter. Until then, she had not ventured further than France.

The remainder of our time in Bangkok was filled with other such charming delights. We never again resorted to McDonald's, but instead discovered a little restaurant in the supermarket that was just down the road from our hotel.

Here we sat alongside the locals, perched on stools at the counter, and watched the chefs as they worked. The menu was entirely in Thai, which was not a language any of us understood, so we just decided what meals looked most delicious and pointed to them as they were delivered to one of our fellow diners! Of course we had to eat with chopsticks, no fancy cutlery here, but we managed. Even little Lucy got the hang of them after a little while.

It never really occurred to my husband or me that perhaps at such a tender age, Lucy would have difficulty coping with the transition, adjusting to life in a strange new place with different foods and customs than those of her homeland.

We got lucky; the only thing that ever made her a little uneasy was when the stallholders in the street markets (which we frequented several times to buy silk ties, clothes, and fake designer watches) touched her hair. They were apparently fascinated by such a pretty little fair-haired child, as their own children were mostly dark-haired.

She put up with the heat, the crowded streets, the unusual sights and smells. She posed with all the huge golden statues at the Grand Palace, looking very cute in the brightly-coloured short and t-shirt sets emblazoned with elephant embroidery that we had acquired in the street markets. She loved a little mechanical dog we bought her and played with it constantly in our hotel room, wearing out the batteries as she sent it marching back and forth across the carpet.

We went to a dancing show where she was entranced by the beautiful little dancers, some barely bigger than she was. They wore colourful, exotic costumes and moved with such grace. It was so wonderful to see all these things through her little eyes.

We rode in tuk-tuks, imagining that we were risking life and limb every time the drivers of these festively decorated little machines hurtled around corners or weaved their way through the busy traffic.

All in all it was a wonderful adventure, so wonderful that we decided to do a stopover there again on our return to England at the end of the year.

I have been back to Bangkok several times since then and have had a fabulous time, a different kind of time now that Lucy is fully grown. Sadly she doesn't remember very much at all about that first trip. Travel such as this is probably a little wasted on a two-year-old, although I am firmly of the opinion that it established a seed in her; she is now a great traveller.

From Thailand, we travelled to Hong Kong. Quite a different proposition, particularly as the country was in something of an unsettling situation. They were awaiting the handover of their island colony back to mainland China.

It was 1997, and that year was signalling the end of 156 years of British rule.

It was a strange time; most of the locals I spoke to were very anxious about it and the wealthier ones had already started making plans to leave—getting residency and passports for other countries like the USA and Canada. People were fearful for their livelihoods, especially those who ran businesses that did not depend on Chinese imports.

While roaming the streets, visiting the night markets, going on the Star Ferry and up in the cable car to the Peak, the story was the same. Everyone was nervous; the Hong Kong they had known all their lives was about to change. No one quite knew what to expect when their country was given back to the Chinese after being a British Colony for 156 years.

The t-shirt my husband bought at the Stanley Market said it all. It was a white t-shirt that featured a large pair of red chopsticks with the words, "*The Great Chinese Takeaway.*"

Regardless of the events of the world at the time, we had a wonderful visit in Hong Kong. We explored and ate delicious food, and little Lucy got to become even more skilled with her chopsticks!

After Hong Kong, we were due to spend a few days in Sydney.

My first trip to Australia had been some 10 years earlier, but this was my first trip to Sydney. This was in the days long before the internet made hotel booking easy, but I was fairly confident in my ability to choose well. Sadly, I did not choose well. I had picked a small, inexpensive hotel in Kings Cross, which turned out to be—back in 1997–a rather uninspiring and run down area of Sydney. Still, we could easily get by without a few luxuries!

The hotel had no restaurant on site, so early the next morning (5:30 am to be precise, as our two-year-old kept fairly unsociable hours) my husband and daughter ventured out to find some breakfast.

Returning a half hour later and proudly clutching her McDonald's breakfast (they were the only café open at that ungodly hour), she announced something very exciting that had happened on their outing.

"*Mum, there were lots of ladies in sparkly dresses standing outside the clubs and they all smiled at me and Dad.*"

My husband later told me that the ladies in sparkly dresses were all ladies of the night, and the clubs were strip joints!

The rest of our Sydney trip was not quite as exciting as that morning walk for Lucy and my husband, although I do have fond memories of her hopping with kangaroos at the zoo!

From Sydney we travelled to Auckland, New Zealand, the place that was going to be our home for the next year. I had no idea at that time that it would play such a big part in the rest of our lives. In 1997, the move was just meant to be a little adventure, something we could do as a family before Lucy started school.

Our new home was in Albany, on the North Shore of New Zealand.

Driving over the Harbour Bridge, looking at the sparkling water of the Hauraki Gulf and the bustle of yachts and boats of all sizes, I could see why it was known as the City of Sails.

At that time, Albany was almost in the country, a quiet, rural place surrounded by farms and fruit orchards. It suited us well, as our home in England was a quiet little country village.

My husband taught in a local school, so Lucy and I would drop him off there in the mornings and spend the day exploring our new home. We also joined children's music groups and made new friends.

It was a wonderful, glorious year.

We spent our weekends travelling the length and breadth of the country.

We visited all the tourist sights and admired the spectacular scenery.

Our family loved the South Island. We discovered how quickly one could leave the cities and towns behind to suddenly find quiet rural roads with barely another car in sight. We saw penguins and seals on remote beaches and marvelled at the wingspan of the model birds at the Albatross Centre. I understood how ancient mariners had held these huge birds in such awe.

Travelling around the country we saw mighty rivers, mountains, volcanoes, old gold mining towns, hot pools, and geysers. We learnt about maraes, moko, and the rich Māori history. We saw sophisticated cosmopolitan cities, stunning scenery, and sunny, spectacular beaches with hardly anyone else in view. We learnt about sausage sizzles, jandals, and gardens that grew almost overnight.

New Zealand was such a different world from the one we left behind. Together, we decided that one day, hopefully within a year or two, we would permanently swap our English lives for this new and exciting place on the other side of the world.

DAY TRIPS TO FRANCE

When you live in southeast England, day trips to France are perfectly possible. Back in the 1990s these were incredibly popular—known as booze runs!

The idea was that you set out early, catching a ferry from Dover to Calais.

Once the Channel Tunnel was built it became even easier; you just drove to Folkestone, put your car on the train and crossed underneath the English Channel for 31 miles, emerging out from the dark tunnel into wide open roads that led you directly into Calais town.

Calais is located in northern France. It originated as a fishing village and is now a major cross-channel port handling millions of cars, passengers, and freight every year.

It is also a place full of history—the Battle of Crécy, the Hundred Years' War, Napoleon.

I would always go on these trips with a few girlfriends. We all had children, so it was a real luxury to have a day off; if we were lucky we managed to go twice a year. We always went on weekdays, leaving home at five in the morning so the kids' dads were responsible for getting them dressed, breakfasted, and ready for school. Neither our husbands nor our children minded this, for they knew we would come home laden with treasures.

Our first stop was always Cité Europe, a huge modern shopping complex built close to the Eurotunnel terminal. We would browse in the dress shops, have a coffee and croissant, and then go to the huge hypermarkets—Auchan and Carrefour. We would spend hours wandering the aisles of these enormous stores buying clothing, stationery, food, and wine. I was also rather fond of the enormous plastic bottles of lavender linen spray, and cloth slippers especially designed for wearing when washing your tiled floors! Everything seemed so much more exciting when the labels were in French. One time while there, I even bought a bike for my daughter! There were always tarte aux pommes, baguettes, delicious biscuits, chocolate, and smelly French cheeses in my shopping trolley too.

Then there was the wine, the main reason for our trip. At that time, it was so much cheaper to pop over the Channel and stock up on your favourite beverages. The wine that I paid five pounds for in England could be snapped up in Calais for a third of the price. I stacked my trolley high with boxes and boxes of Côtes Du Rhône and an occasional bottle or two of white or sparkling wine thrown in for good measure. There were limits on how much one was allowed to take back into England without being charged duty on their purchases, so we were always careful not to overindulge.

After splurging, it was back into the car for a drive along the coast road, the D940, past Sangatte and Wissant, eventually reaching our destination of Wimereux, a little seaside town some three miles north of Boulogne. We would park the car, stroll along the long sandy beach, then meander our way through the narrow streets, admiring the rather unusual architecture. We gazed at the colourful houses with towers, turrets, gables, and balconies. We wandered the main street, Rue Carnot, admiring all the stock in the little independent shops that lined the street. If it was market day, we would perhaps be tempted to buy more bread, or maybe a little fruit.

Like many French towns, Wimereux is full of history.

At the Commonwealth War Graves Cemetery, there is a stone marking the grave of John McCrae, who in 1915 wrote the evocative poem "*In Flanders Fields*."

Having seen and done everything on our lists, we headed to the Hôtel De Wimereux for lunch. It was a simple, typical French hotel restaurant, always full of locals who were there to enjoy the plat du jour.

The food was delicious, as was the rather attractive waiter who always insisted on treating us strange English women to free apéritifs, desserts, or exotic liqueurs. No wonder we returned time after time to his restaurant!

I have so many other stories of time spent over the years in France, but I will include these in later chapters.

VENICE

Venice, dear Venice, one of my favourite, most-loved destinations.

The first time I visited was for my 50th birthday.

My husband had no desire to go, so I persuaded four girlfriends to go with me.

We caught the last flight from London and arrived late at night. Unfortunately one of our suitcases didn't arrive with us, so after reporting it and spending ages hanging around, when we finally emerged from the old airport right by the water's edge, it was completely deserted. All the water taxis and vaporettos (water buses) had departed. We were alone, with no way of getting to Venice. Fortunately, one in our group, Manuela, was Italian, so she went to the telephone box to seek help. Ignoring all the business cards on the walls offering us massages, Italian lessons, and assorted other delights, she managed to find a number for a taxi service. After a while, a rather grumpy old gentleman with his pyjamas showing underneath his overcoat appeared and offered to drive us to Piazzale Roma. From there, he assured us we would have time to catch the last vaporetto.

He was right. We clambered onto the water bus, dragging our heavy suitcases, and managed to find a spot on the outside deck. It was freezing, one o'clock in the morning on a wintry March night, and a cold wind was blowing across the lagoon.

The vaporetto crisscrossed the Grand Canal, picking up hotel and restaurant workers and delivering them to their home destinations.

By this point, we were pretty exhausted and a little stressed. We had absolutely no idea where we should disembark. It was pitch black outside, and only a few of the buildings were lit up. Every time we saw a palace or large church, we were convinced this must be our stop. Finally we recognised the Doge's Palace and St. Mark's Basilica. We got off the vaporetto near the Bridge of Sighs and dragged our suitcases along cobbled streets, up and down old stone steps. By now we were getting pretty desperate; we only had three days in Venice and at this rate, we were never even going to find our hotel!

Suddenly we turned a corner into St. Mark's Square. It was completely empty, just us five women and the moonlight, and it was a sight I will never forget. It was at this moment that I fell under the spell of this majestic city. That feeling has never left me, despite visiting Venice at least another half a dozen times over the years.

That first visit was truly wonderful. We saw so much.

We climbed the 323 steps of the Campanile to take in marvellous views of the city and the lagoon. We queued with all the other tourists to admire the splendours inside Basilica di San Marco. We wandered the streets, getting hopelessly lost, arguing over exactly which bridge we should have crossed. We visited the Gallerie dell'Accademia, where I fell in love with huge old paintings by Vittore Carpaccio. I was fascinated to learn that some of the paintings in the gallery had originally been in private homes and had been cut to fit around doorways. That gallery is a must see if you are in Venice and have a little time to spare.

We ate at little backstreet restaurants; often we were the only tourists there, which appealed to my adventurous streak. We heard stories of the annual Carnevale, held just a few weeks earlier, and I put that on my future wish list. How wonderful it would be to don a glamorous costume and mask, and mingle with the locals in the misty February alleyways? Sadly, I still have yet to achieve that ambition.

We visited some of the marvellous costume shops dotted around the city, all stocked to the brim with fabulous masks and costumes. We drank Prosecco at eleven in the morning and popped into the famous Harry's Bar for a Peach Bellini.

We visited the Rialto market, marvelling at all the fresh fruit, vegetables, and fish. We shopped for Parmesan cheese in a little shop just behind the Ponte Di Rialto. We bought pizza from a fast food restaurant by the canal, queuing for ages with all the locals buying their lunch.

We shopped of course, buying the obligatory masks, leather handbags, and bags of brightly-coloured dry pasta, some looking like coloured liquorice or black and white bows. I found a watch, the face made from Millefiori, as you may find in glass paperweights. Having been a collector of paperweights for more than twenty years (a habit acquired in my teens, of which you can learn more if you are interested in my memoirs *FROM THERE TO HERE, WITH AN AWFUL LOT IN BETWEEN),* these appealed to me hugely. Ideally I would have loved to purchase some beautiful Murano glass vases or paperweights, but these were way out of my price range. I contented myself instead with a 10 euro watch. Actually, I ended up buying four of these watches—all for myself I am ashamed to say—and on later visits to Venice I think I may have even indulged in a few more!

Perhaps this is a good moment to mention my suitcase addiction.

I am not altogether certain when it actually started; I suspect it was some time in my late thirties or early forties. Having not been able to afford holidays as a child, I think I probably equate having lots of luggage with being able to travel to exotic places.

It started simply enough.

I was on holiday and I had done rather too much shopping, as usual. There was no way it would all fit into my suitcase, so I ended up buying another large, squashy bag that could double up as hand luggage.

When I first started travelling in earnest, things seemed much easier. Perhaps that is the rosy glow of memories tarnished by time, but we certainly didn't seem to have to worry so much about hand luggage then.

In the early days I often boarded a return flight laden down with huge and heavy parcels, and was never stopped from taking them on board. Now of course, it is quite different. We all have to weigh and re-weigh our luggage, ensuring it will not tip over the airline's accepted limits. In many ways, this has taken away the spontaneity of shopping whilst abroad. Nowadays, unless you are wealthy and can afford to ship items, you get stuck in the awful position of having to leave behind a huge carpet, china statue, or massive painting because you do not have any room in your luggage. In my experience, those things you fell in love with on your travels but weren't able to squeeze in your overflowing suitcase will always be elusive memories, dreams of what might have been!

But I digress, probably because I want to avoid the embarrassment of admitting to my addiction. Over the years I must have bought at least thirty new suitcases and holdalls—some full sized, some smaller hand luggage, and several squashy ones of assorted sizes. These squashy ones, I reasoned, were particularly useful for any unexpected purchases, as they could be stored inside my main suitcase, only to be removed in case of need.

I have bought luggage from many destinations, much to the dismay of any travelling companions at the time. *"Pat, do you really need another bag? Can't you manage with what you've got? You've got loads at home already. It's just a waste of money!"*

Suffice to say I never listen. My suitcase supply continued to increase over the years, as I would often discover yet another perfect one to add to the collection.

"This one is surely the answer to all my prayers. See how it expands?"

"And this small case on wheels is definitely superior to the one I bought last year; see how easily it twirls on its four sturdy little wheels? It will be so easy to handle at the airport."

"All my other ones are boring old black, very hard to identify on the baggage carousel. This bright red one will be much better.

Oh hang on, what about this highly patterned one? I certainly won't lose that!"

Over the years I graduated from one small blue suitcase to a matching set, all of which had to be carried by hand—no wheeled ones for me in those early years. Then there were lots of boring ones, some in reinforced nylon, some were canvas, and there were even a couple of hard shell ones.

Like a magpie, I then graduated to coloured cases, cases on wheels, cases with pictures and emblems! At one time I had a whole set of beautiful red luggage pieces and was sure I had found my perfect set at last. However, they soon got tatty, being thrown on and off airport conveyor belts, so I briefly returned to boring black ones, personalising them with coloured ribbons on the handles. For a while I used luggage straps. I had some rather splendid straps with rainbow stripes and even a set with my surname on them, but this proved to be a short term experiment as they were forever getting lost… secured to the case while embarking and missing on arrival.

Now I am content with some rather stylish French luggage in a fetching shade of dark brown. They must be made of some super fabric; they seem to be surviving all the rigours that long haul travel throws at them. They still look pretty decent even after many years of wear.

Still, I do not think this habit is controlled. I cannot pass a luggage shop without popping in. I stroke the cases, test out their wheels and wonder. Perhaps one day I'll need a change from my brown bags, perfect as they are now!

Fortunately in this way, the Covid pandemic has stopped me in my tracks a little. I am not able to plan any trips and as yet, I have managed to refrain from buying any new luggage online. But I cannot promise you this will last. After all, I am only 70 years old—I will almost certainly need another suitcase or two before I depart on my final journey!

THE FRENCH COUNTRYSIDE

As I have said, living in England made travel throughout Europe very easy.

I had already visited Paris several times, once getting horribly lost on the Périphérique, the enormous circular highway surrounding the city.

I had driven down country to the Dordogne region, via the Loire Valley, stopping en route to admire the city of Orleans, home of Joan of Arc. Here I drank delicious white wine, a speciality of the region.

I had visited Périgueux, Bergerac, Ribérac, Sarlat-la-Canéda, Terrasson-Lavilledieu, and Brantôme. I had seen beautiful chateaux, caves, and rivers, and sunbathed on pine-fringed west Atlantic beaches with enormous sand dunes. I had bought large plastic bottles full of red wine from small winemakers, wine that somehow tasted far better than that from a bottle bought in a supermarket. I had eaten enough delicious baguettes and croissants to sink a battleship, visited more markets than you could count, and gone to the mountains several times for ski trips.

When our friends Sam and India moved to France, we visited them almost every summer until we emigrated to New Zealand. They were living in the Charente Maritime, in a small village an hour or so from La Rochelle.

Those were glorious times. Our daughters were the same age, so it was easy to find things to occupy both of our families.

When we visited, we stayed with them in their beautiful old stone house, deep in the French countryside and surrounded by fields full of sunflowers. They took us to beaches, markets, and lovely restaurants. We often went to Fouras, a charming seaside town, and I was always amazed that, although we never arrived there until the late afternoon, neither did many of the locals. It was much too hot to spend all day under the August sun. After sunbathing on the sandy beach for a while and watching our girls enjoy swimming in the warm sea, we would picnic on the beach, enjoying a delicious concoction of jambon baguettes and frites! Then we would wander to the night market, soaking up the atmosphere and making a small purchase or two. On one particular occasion, there was a night concert in the main square and I was enthralled by the tall Mongolian throat singer. It made me want to go to Mongolia in search of more. Russia was already on my wish list, but until that point I hadn't really considered any of its surrounding countries.

Over the years we visited all the local sights, La Rochelle, Bordeaux, and St. Émillion, where Lucy and I enjoyed touring the vineyards.

I loved the city of Bordeaux, the wide boulevards, the architecture, the white stone buildings, the history. We visited a fascinating little museum there, dedicated to the brave French

Resistance fighters, and it was sobering to read of their dangerous exploits and see remnants of that dreadful time. The museum featured artifacts from the time, including the blue and white striped uniforms from the death camps.

We often went to the Île de Ré, a charming island just off the Atlantic coast. One summer, the girls insisted on driving ‘round and ‘round the island, as they had heard that Johnny Depp owned a house there and they were keen to see him!

We enjoyed long lazy lunches in a lovely restaurant by the harbour—delicious prawns and moules-frites washed down with local wine—before wandering around the market to buy linen dresses, leather shoes, and artisan soaps.

We also visited the Île d’Oléron, the largest island on the French Atlantic coast. I was fascinated by the sea salt industry there. There were salt marshes and oyster shacks all over, and everywhere you drove there were huge bags of salt by the roadside, just waiting to be purchased. I bought a small bag of this salt, together with a rather nice china salt pot that I still use to this day.

On our travels one day, we popped into an ordinary little supermarket in a small and uninspiring town, where I was thrilled to discover beautiful blue shell-patterned china. I liked it so much that I returned to England with 42 pieces of it in my hand luggage!

We went to Cognac and sampled fine brandy. We enjoyed delicious cakes and ice creams. We ate in little cafes, bars, and fine restaurants. Our girls absorbed all that France had to offer. They rode the carousel at the beach, visited water parks, went fishing, and collected snails in the early evening after a rainfall.

Hopefully the world will reopen one day (this memoir is being written during a global pandemic), and I will be able to visit again. I still need to see the lavender fields in Provence, as well as a multitude of other places.

AROUND THE WORLD AGAIN AND BACK TO MY BELOVED FIJI

In 2006, we decided to go around the world again. It had been a long 10 years since we had last done such a trip and I was so excited at the prospect.

We planned to go for six weeks and Lucy wanted to take her best friend, Kemba, along with us.

We had a marvellous time. We were more seasoned travellers by this point; I didn't make the same rookie mistakes, such as booking accommodations in dodgy areas! It was lovely to retrace our footsteps as well as discover new places, and it was a wonderful experience for two teenage girls.

We visited Singapore, had afternoon tea at Raffles Hotel, shopped, and absorbed all the sights the city had to offer. I dragged the girls around Chinatown and bored them with stories of my previous visit. I even took them out to Haw Par Villa, where the concrete effigies of Hell left a lasting impression on them!

In Sydney we enjoyed staying in a hotel right on Darling Harbour, and again I dragged them around the city, either on the monorail or the hop on/hop off buses. I was so anxious, trying to make sure they did not miss a thing and that they made memories to last a lifetime, just in case they never had a chance to return.

We went on to New Zealand which was exciting, but rather bittersweet, as I was still longing to emigrate there. It had been twelve long years since we left, and as soon as I stepped back on NZ soil I realised it was where I wanted to be. Time had done nothing to change my mind.

We revisited old haunts, saw old friends, and travelled the entire length and breadth of the beautiful country. I was incredibly sad when it was time to leave, but felt sure that it would not be long before we returned for good.

The next stop was the highlight of the trip for me—a return to my beloved Fiji.

I had not been since 1987, an absence of almost 20 years. With today's technology—global internet, Facebook, Skype, Zoom, and the like, that perhaps doesn't seem such a big issue. However, communication across oceans certainly wasn't so easy back then.

I had missed so much of my Fijian family's lives, births, marriages, and deaths.

I needn't have worried though; in no time at all I was firmly back in the arms of my loved ones, cuddling the new babies and making remarks about how grown up all the "toddlers" I had known back in 1987 now were!

It was wonderful to introduce my husband and my two girls—both Lucy and Kemba—to my extended Fijian family, and equally wonderful to see that in no time at all, they too had fallen a little in love with Fiji and its people.

We cruised to the beautiful Yasawa islands and wandered on pristine sandy beaches, once in a while dipping into the warm clear ocean where little fish nibbled at our toes. The rest of my family went snorkelling on the reef and came back with tales of glorious schools of brightly-coloured fish, coral, and even the occasional shark. Not being much of a water lover myself, I had been quite content to simply stroll on the long sandy beach, a beach I had almost entirely to myself. I watched in awe as hundreds of little creatures in their beautiful exotic shells ran across the land in front of me. It was one of those truly magical moments, a bit like being in an episode of a David Attenborough or National Geographic special.

While in Fiji, we took a cruise. Our ship, a member of the Blue Lagoon fleet, was quite a small boat—just 34 cabins. We had the chance to get to know our fellow passengers this way, which was lovely. On Christmas Day, the tour leader of the small Japanese group onboard surprised us all by appearing at breakfast wearing a Father Christmas hat along with his business suit (for the whole four days in the 30 degree tropical heat, he never relaxed or wore anything more casual). He presented us all with gifts of macramé birds, lovingly made by his tour guests.

During our trip, I showed my family as much of Fiji as I could, visiting my friends in their own fairly humble homes. I explained to my girls that the lives of our friends were not as monetarily prosperous as the lives they lived at home in England, and it was a lesson well learned. To see the pleasure on the face of a young girl of their own age when she opened her gift containing pencils, pens, erasers, a ruler, a pencil case, and notebooks, made them realise how lucky they were to live where they did. "*Oh, vinaka vakalevu (*thank you); *my friends will all think I am the richest girl in the school with all these new things.*"

Our trip to Fiji changed all our lives.

A DIFFERENT KIND OF SPAIN

It was many years before I ventured back to Spain. There was so much of the world to see, so many places that seemed more exotic and were further afield.

Then, my friend Valerie suggested a little trip there to see her sister, who lived in the mountains above Marbella on the Costa de Sol.

As you now know, I love a travel adventure of any kind, so it took no persuading to buy me a ticket.

We flew to Málaga and picked up a hire car at the airport. We were trying to make it an economical trip, so we had chosen the smallest car available—a little Fiat, I think.

As you may have noticed, I am not very knowledgeable or interested in cars. I will almost always refer to them simply by their colour, or perhaps by the manufacturer's name if I am really paying attention. I have owned some very nice cars in my time, but the only ones I am really passionate about are the first one I owned, a 1957 Morris Minor 1000, and the one I currently drive, a beaten up old Nissan X-Trail, which is a bit like a tank! Although, I was also rather excited about a shiny red open-top sports car I was lucky enough to own for a few years. There is nothing quite like driving 'round country lanes with the wind blowing in your hair.

So, suffice to say, I am not particularly interested in the engine or workings of any car. To me it is merely a vehicle, a way of getting from points A to B, hopefully without breaking down. I apologise to all you car enthusiasts out there who probably think I am pretty ignorant in that department!

Anyway, we picked up the car and I was the designated driver; although Valerie was an excellent driver with many years of experience, the hire company ruled that her age excluded her.

Driving along the busy motorway towards Marbella, we soon realised that the tank was running low. We needed petrol, so we stopped at the nearest service station and I got out to fill up the tank. Standing in my little summer dress and open-toed sandals, looking around at the scenery, I didn't bother to check the pump to see how much the fuel would cost us. It was only a little car, so surely it would be quite cheap to run, right? Suddenly, I felt my feet getting splashed and looked down to see petrol pouring out of the pump, all over the forecourt. The tiny petrol tank was full and here I was, trying to squeeze more into it!

It was very embarrassing, particularly as I then tried to apologise to the forecourt attendant in my extremely inadequate and therefore perfectly useless Spanish.

That aside, a lesson was learned and has never been repeated since. The rest of our journey along the coast was enjoyable and overall, pretty uneventful.

We arrived at our all-inclusive hotel to find it full of mostly Spanish families, all enjoying the sun. Valerie's sister, Sylvia, owned a clothing boutique at that time and she was holding a fashion show around the pool. Within minutes we were both wearing some of her creations, strutting our stuff and hoping to entice the holidaymakers to make some purchases.

That hotel was such fun. They had lovely swimming pools, music, friendly staff, and the most gigantic buffets I have ever seen. It is very hard to be sensible with your diet when you are presented on a daily basis with such delights for breakfast, morning tea, lunch, and dinner!

One evening, we joined the Spanish families sitting outside on the vast terrace to play Bingo. It was quite an adventure. I am not very experienced at this game, but I was surrounded by people who were. Even Valerie had a whole handful of cards to play, meanwhile I could barely keep up with watching one card—especially as the numbers were called out in Spanish.

After the games were finished, the compère announced that a late supper was available in the small dining room. There was a rush as some of the families around us leapt up from their chairs. We sat there for a while, nursing our drinks, still full from eating too much at dinnertime. Eventually though, we decided that perhaps we should check out the excitement, too.

It was now midnight, but the little dining room was crowded. Hordes of children (it was late, but that is the European way... siesta during the hot afternoons, then party at night) were making themselves snacks. Huge hot dogs dripping with ketchup and mustard, hot potato chips, big slabs of cake.

We looked at each other. How could these kids possibly manage to eat any more?

We had watched in fascination earlier in the day at the size of the portions they already enjoyed at breakfast, lunch, and dinner.

Then, with absolutely no concern that we might end up the size of some of these voluptuous Spanish ladies, we found ourselves making hot dogs. They tasted pretty good, too!

The rest of that trip was such fun.

We visited wholesalers, huge warehouses stacked high with boxes of clothing direct from China. It was clothing that could be bought in bulk very cheaply, then be resold in shops around the world for much higher prices.

We ate delicious tapas in little backstreet bars. We drove up high into the mountains and ate dinner al fresco at a lovely restaurant. I popped into a tiny pharmacy and, in very broken Spanish, managed to buy mosquito repellent and water retention tablets to cure my swollen ankles.

We visited the fabulous market in Marbella, where I bought kaftans, scarves, and leather shoes galore. My favourites were a pair of lime-green loafers, which I wore for many summers after that. Clearly, they were a good investment.

We approached a famous bull ring and I was glad that it was closed; I could just look at the colourful advertising posters this way, rather than having to watch the rather barbaric spectacle myself.

Valerie and I went on a wonderful boat trip to Puerto Banús, and I wished there had been enough time to take a day trip to nearby Gibraltar.

In just a few days, I had seen enough to convince me that Spain was indeed a country I should explore further, so Barcelona, Madrid, Granada, Seville, Cádiz, Pamplona, and many other cities were added to my bucket list.

THE DEEP SOUTH

Even the journey was an adventure.

My first time in the Deep South of America was to attend the wedding of an old friend who had emigrated from the UK a few years earlier.

She had always described Huntsville as a "hick town," so I was expecting something dry and dusty, a rural backwater. Oh, how wrong I was.

But first, the trip there.

There were no direct flights to the town, so my 14-year-old daughter and I flew from London to Chicago. We had a lengthy stopover there but it didn't matter, there was so much to see just in the airport terminal. Even airport newsstands are more interesting when you are abroad.

The airport was full of young men and their families; the men were all in military uniforms, awaiting their flights to Afghanistan to fight the Taliban. Some of them looked so young and my heart went out to their mothers, who were obviously trying not to cry.

Our internal flight, booked with United Airlines but operated by American Eagle, was a surprise.

As we boarded the tiny plane with just one seat on each side of the aisle and probably less than 30 seats in total, we were greeted by a charming blonde flight attendant who had probably celebrated her 60th birthday a decade or more earlier.

She was very sweet, anxious that we found our seats comfortable, and most apologetic that she would not be serving us food on the short flight.

This woman was the only crew apart from the captain and his second-in-command. It seemed that she had been flying this route forever, as many of the other passengers—mostly businessmen—seemed to know her.

After take-off, she came round with the drinks trolley.

"What would you like, honey?"

My teenage daughter had never been referred to as "honey" before, but I could tell she quite liked it.

"May I have water, please?"

"Sorry, what did you want, honey?"

"Water please."

"Oh, you mean Waa… ter."

"Honey, I just love your British accent. It's so cute."

Our friend Michelle picked us up at the airport in her enormous tank-like car, and I was stunned when we pulled out onto the wide freeway. This was nothing like the hick town I had been expecting.

Huntsville, Alabama, also known as Rocket City, is the home of the U.S. Space and Rocket Center. Lining the freeway as we drove along were enormous rockets, absolutely not what I had expected to see.

Michelle's house was almost a mansion by English standards, a beautiful brick built house with columns, pillars, and a sweeping staircase set in an acre of gardens. Her street was lined with similar houses, all with immaculate lawns and well-tended plants. It was early May, so the extreme summer heat had not yet quite kicked in, although I still found it pretty stifling.

For the whole week we stayed there I only met one of her neighbours, a delightful Black lady whose beautiful children were going to be bridal attendants at the wedding. She lived in the house next door and I really enjoyed her company. We chatted for ages and she told me stories of her late grandmother, who had been born into slavery there in Alabama.

I never saw any other neighbours at all; apparently they just went from their air-conditioned homes into their huge integral garages, got into their huge air-conditioned cars, and drove to their air-conditioned offices or the mall.

It was a very busy week. There was a lot of wedding planning to do and of course, that involved shopping!

I soon learnt to navigate my way around Walmart, Costco, TJMaxx, and other such delights. We ate at some fun restaurants and drank plenty of margaritas. We travelled to the wedding in the biggest stretch limo I had ever seen and learnt to salsa—the groom was Cuban. For brunch the following day, I learnt how to make "*grits,*" "*biscuits,*" and to scramble 45 eggs at the same time!

On my second trip to Huntsville a few years later, Michelle drove me on a tour of the surrounding area. I was a bit disappointed not to see any cotton in the fields, apparently I was too early. Instead, she took me to a little gift shop in the old part of town where I was able to buy a small cotton ball, still attached to the stem. I was very excited to have this—the whole cotton picking industry had always fascinated me—but sadly, when I declared it at customs on my return to New Zealand (and despite it being in a hermetically sealed bag), they declared it was a possible biosecurity hazard and confiscated it!

I loved the old part of Huntsville. I was intrigued by all the old photos, especially the ones from the early 1900s showing the Courthouse Square, wagons loaded down with cotton waiting to be sold. I was sad to read that splendid old buildings like the Elks Theater and the Carnegie Library had been demolished in the 1960s in the name of "progress," although I was glad to see that other notable buildings had been renovated and turned into offices. I also learnt that in the early 1900s, Huntsville had several large mills to process some of the cotton grown in the fields.

There are still some splendid old antebellum-style houses in Huntsville—think Gone With The Wind—and I was delighted to visit the Burritt Museum, an art-deco home built in the shape of a Maltese cross with bales of straw in the walls as insulation! This house is located on Round Top Mountain and has spectacular views of the surrounding countryside. Another interesting little fact is that Huntsville was once known as the "watercress capital of the world," and during the winter months supplied well over half the needs of the American market.

Founded in 1805, it seems that Huntsville brought many "firsts" to the state of Alabama—the first bank, the first public library, and the first cotton mill.

If you get the chance to visit this fascinating place, it will certainly be worth your while.

NEW YORK, NEW YORK

New York, New York! So good I went there twice.

After attending Michelle's wedding in Alabama, it seemed like a good idea for Lucy and me to stop over there for a few days on our way back to England. She was just 14 years old and it was her first visit to the States. Although I had been to California and Florida several times, this would be my first visit to the Big Apple, too.

What fun we had!

We stayed in a little boutique hotel just off Times Square and wandered the streets all day every day, desperate to see as much of the exciting city as we possibly could in the short time frame we had. Much to my teenage daughter's annoyance, I also insisted we used the Hop-on/Hop-off tourist buses as I quickly realised this was by far the best way to see the city.

We packed so much into those few days—sightseeing, shopping, The Lion King on Broadway, Central Park, Harlem, delicious shrimp at Bubba Gump's, the Staten Island Ferry, the Empire State Building, and lots of smoked salmon bagels. When we left, we were determined to return.

And return we did the very next year. This time, I was in the company of three of Lucy's best friends. Four 15-year-old girls. I can hear you mutter, "Is this woman completely mad? Who in their right mind would voluntarily take four teenage girls to New York for a week?"

Guilty as charged. But there was a kind of logic to my plan. I was trying to soften the blow a little, to make up for the fact that we were about to drag my daughter, our only child, to a new home across the world. Our residence visas for New Zealand had been granted, so it would only be a matter of time before these friendships were left behind. In the meantime, memories had to be made!

On arrival at JFK airport, the girls were thrilled to see a very handsome Black man brandishing a sign with Lucy's name on it. He led us across the carpark and I heard a squeal as the girls saw the car they would be travelling to the city in.

"*OMG, it's a Hummer.*"

I had no idea what a Hummer was; I had just ordered a stretch limo as a treat. However, the girls were very impressed. They were even more impressed when we pulled up to our hotel on East 34th Street and the doorman came out and shook each of them by the hand, welcoming them to New York. He then took us up to our rooms: two huge interconnecting bedrooms with a large lounge separating them. A few minutes later, he was back with special pillows and yoga equipment so that the girls could exercise in the spacious rooms, as they were too young to use the hotel gym.

Wanting them to experience all the luxury the hotel had to offer, I let them use the bedrooms while I slept on the rather uncomfortable sofa bed in the lounge. Such is a mother's love!

We had the most incredible time.

I dragged them to see all the sights. We queued for ages in the foyer of the Empire State Building and then spent hours at the top, soaking in all the fabulous views. They loved the bright lights of Times Square, window shopping on Fifth Avenue—Tiffany's, Macy's, Saks, and Cartier, all the places they had seen on TV shows and movies.

I dragged them through Chinatown and then into SoHo, where they were very happy to stop for a coffee in the trendy area.

I persuaded them to do the late-night Brooklyn Bus Tour, which was fun and informative but exceedingly cold on a chilly March evening.

We went to Harlem, Central Park, and Queens, and I insisted on pointing out all the fabulous architecture I had so admired on my previous visit: the Flatiron Building, City Hall, the Chrysler Building, the Dakota (where John Lennon was shot), the Woolworth Building, Radio City Music Hall, and the Waldorf Astoria.

I even dragged them to the parade on Fifth Avenue on Easter Sunday to see all the fabulous bonnets. Here, they took great delight in teasing me as I openly admired an attractive tall Black man who was looking very stylish in camel-coloured cashmere—from his Fedora hat to his ankle-length coat and very expensive shiny gold shoes.

One of the days, we went on a trip to see the Statue of Liberty.

It was a cold day, so we sat inside the boat as it sped across the harbour towards Lady Liberty. Did you know that she stands 93 metres tall, has an almost 11 metre waistline, and has 25 windows in her crown? No? Neither did I.

It was a shock to see just how enormous and imposing she really was; photos do her no justice. In real life she is an awesome sight, and I could only wonder what those early immigrants must have thought when she was the first thing they saw as they approached their new home in America.

I was very keen to get off the boat when it stopped at Ellis Island, but by then the girls had had enough culture for one day and just wanted to get back to the warmth and excitement of the city. I went out onto the deck alone to look at the buildings that, for more than sixty years, had processed new immigrants.

I found it all very emotional. There was a man standing on the deck next to me with two small boys.

We chatted.

"*My grandparents came from Italy and passed through here. I want my kids to know what their ancestors went through to give us the life we have today, but I don't suppose they will ever really understand. Life is so easy for young people these days.*"

I looked at my girls, snuggled up inside the warmth of the boat, seemingly unmoved by all the human emotion, suffering, and history that place had seen.

I agreed. We decided that history is wasted on those too young to really appreciate it.

Our week in New York passed in a flash. We had a wonderful time, but I am quite sure that if the girls recorded all their memories of the trip, they would be a little different from mine!

WHY DON'T WE EMIGRATE TO THE SOUTHERN HEMISPHERE?

You may recall that following our year's sabbatical to New Zealand in 1996, it had been our intention to emigrate there.

Sadly, circumstances and my husband's lack of enthusiasm meant that it took us another 14 long years to make that intention a reality. By this time I had almost given up hope of ever returning to the place where I felt so at home, where I truly believed we could make a better life for our little family.

If you are interested in learning more about this move, I have written about it extensively in my memoir, "*From There to Here, With An Awful Lot in Between,*" so I will not go into it all again here. Suffice to say that returning to Auckland permanently in 2010 was a very joyful time for me.

As a family we explored all the places we had missed seeing before. This time there was no urgency, as we had the rest of our lives to explore our new adopted country.

ROAD TRIPS IN NEW ZEALAND

We have now travelled to Whakarewarewa Village, or "*the Living Māori Village,*" as it is described in the guidebooks.

I was so excited as I crossed the bridge into this village, where, for over two hundred years, people of the Tūhourangi Ngāti Wāhiao have welcomed visitors from around the world. I had especially wanted to go here, as opposed to some of the other, glitzier tourist attractions in Rotorua. At that time, in 2007, the village was still relatively unspoilt, much as it had been for the last 100 years.

After wandering around the geothermal landscape featuring hot spring lakes, bubbling mud pools, and geysers that, in my imagination, reminded me of the moon's surface, we stopped to enjoy a piece of corn on the cob. It was "*a unique taste of kai* (food), *cooked in our largest hot pool.*"

Watching the traditional dance performances featuring poi (soft, hand-held ball attached to a string) patu (a short club made of wood, whalebone, or pounamu—greenstone), rākau (wooden sticks), taiaha, and much eye-rolling and sticking out of tongues, I was particularly fascinated by one of the tall, fierce, male Māori dancers. It was easy to imagine his warrior ancestors doing the same Haka before going into battle.

Later that day I saw him at the local Warehouse store, buying a toy cricket set for his_kids. I think there is always something rather magical about seeing any kind of performer living their "real" life. They become a more three-dimensional creature, someone with artistic talent, yet still so human!

Over the years, I have come to love the unique smell of the city of Rotorua. Many people find it offensive—rather like rotten eggs due to the hydrogen sulphide, but I, like many of the people who have lived with it all their lives, rather enjoy the smell.

Any kind of road trip in New Zealand is pretty unique.

As soon as you leave the big cities you find yourself driving through beautiful unspoilt countryside with very little traffic. Old farms and homesteads are nestled into the green hillsides, villages with their Four Square stores or little dairies (small convenience stores) advertise Tip Top ice cream.

Every kilometre you drive brings you new wonders; it's a fine example of nature at its very best. Mountains, ancient forests, beaches, volcanoes, bubbling mud pools, lakes, and rivers. Green fields full of cows and sheep. It's no wonder so many filmmakers have chosen to shoot their blockbuster movies here!

I have had the most divine fish and chips, freshly cooked and beautifully served in so many different places; just to name a couple, there was once at a little boutique cinema in Feilding and another in the small market town in the Manawatu district—a town that has won the award for New Zealand's Most Beautiful Town sixteen times!

Mangonui Fish Shop on the North Island specialises in line-caught fish bought directly off the boats, such as snappers, tarakihi, gurnard, and hapuku. Here, you can sit in the little restaurant right on the water's edge, watching through an open window as your dinner is being cooked while also searching for the stingrays, John Dory, kingfish, bronze whaler sharks, or pods of orcas that often swim by the shop.

There's also the option for something simpler, like the numerous times I have enjoyed eating delicious fish and chips from the paper wrapping whilst sitting on a sandy beach and enjoying the sunset.

A road trip down the West Coast of the South Island began with a flight to Christchurch, a beautiful city, much of which was destroyed by the dreadful earthquake in 2010. A few days exploring this place—the Garden City—were followed by an adventure on the TranzAlpine train, a wonderful journey that took us past snow-capped mountains, frozen rivers, and undulating countryside. Then, we disembarked at Greymouth and picked up a hire car. We strolled along some remote wild West Coast beaches with their black sand and piles of driftwood. Next was a stop at Fox Glacier and remaining firmly on the ground while the rest of our group took a helicopter ride to explore the glacier by foot. I wonder how many more years that will be possible with the continuance of global warming?

We stopped briefly at Ship Creek, down a long, unmade road, hemmed in by native bush. It was almost sunset when we arrived at this deserted beach. What an amazing place—almost prehistoric, with its enormous piles of driftwood, black sand, and lots of kākā birds (large olive parrots) sitting in the trees, emitting their harsh, grating calls. I wish we had had time to take a walk through the ancient kahikatea swamp forest, as apparently it "*provides a glimpse back in time to what much of the West Coast may have looked like, prior to human settlement.*"

Traces of gold and coal mining, timber logging, the Pancake Rock formations, forests, limestone cliffs, canyons, caves, and underground streams, together with a spectacular coastline, make this area an absolute must-see.

Travelling south from Hokitika through native forests with stunning views of mountains and lakes was rather like living in a book of picture postcards. Everywhere you looked, the scenery was spectacular.

So many little highlights:

Magnificent pink and purple lupins on the South Island.

Peonies in Blenheim.

Hamilton Gardens.

Larnach Castle.

Ancient forests.

A New Year's Eve concert in Palmerston North sitting outside at midnight, surrounded by families all soaking up the warmth of the balmy evening.

Bushwalks.

Art Deco in Napier.

Mount Cook.

Arrowtown.

Te Mata Peak.

Sliding down giant sand dunes.

Glorious sandy beaches with hardly anyone in sight.

Muriwai Gannet Colony.

Matakohe Museum, with its fabulous displays of Kauri gum.

The All Blacks.

Hobbiton.

The list is endless. However long I live, I don't think I shall ever be bored living in this beautiful country.

VENICE AND THE ANGEL

Before my second visit to Venice, I read a book called *Miss Garnet's Angel* by Sally Vickers. There had been a review of it in the Sunday Times, and as I had fallen in love with the city on my previous visit the year before, I happily purchased the book.

What a joy it turned out to be!

Beautifully written, it mentioned so many of the places I had seen on my travels, as well as other districts, little squares, and islands I had not yet had time to discover.

My travelling companion for this second trip to Venice, my friend Valerie, was very patient as we hunted for the little church featured in the book.

I was desperate to visit the church Miss Garnet had loved, which was located in the Campo dell'Angelo Raffaele in sestiere Dorsoduro. It was one with ravishing Guardi paintings of Tobias and the Angel.

Eventually we found it, but disappointingly it was closed.

Had I not read the book, I probably never would have insisted on returning the next day. The outside of the building and the surrounding area was pretty uninspiring back in 2002, and there was so much more of the city we still wanted to explore.

But we did return the next day, and much to our delight it was open.

The interior, like so many Venetian churches, was far more intriguing than the rather plain exterior. It was full of marble pillars, lighted candles, and the wonderful painting and statues of Tobias and the Angel that had so inspired Miss Garnet. It inspired me too, and on every succeeding visit to Venice, I will always drag my travel companions there.

My other favourite Venetian church is the Santa Maria Assunta I Gesuiti in the

Cannaregio district. We came upon it by chance, and again it was closed when we first arrived. So, we retired to the little bar opposite to drink Peach Bellinis and flirt with the elderly owner. Italian men are very good for your self-esteem!

This church is truly amazing, both inside and out. Richly decorated in opulent Baroque style, it contains paintings by Tintoretto and Titian and has the most incredible ornate marble columns, some of which are so skilfully carved that they look like draped curtains. On the outside, this enormous, impressive pillared building has huge carvings of the twelve apostles, so large that they can be seen from the surrounding lagoon as you approach the city from the outlying islands.

Talking of islands, I must mention our little side trips to Murano, home of the glassblowers, Burano with its colourfully painted houses and lace-making industry, and Torcello, once an important trading centre but now a quiet refuge with an ancient history and a tiny population. I would certainly recommend a trip to all three islands if you have the time!

Back on the mainland, we visited the old Venetian Ghetto, which I was told was one of the oldest ghettos in the world, having been established in 1516.

We went to the Arsenale di Venezia Open Day in the Castello district. We saw models of the doges' magnificent state barge, the Bucintoro, and enjoyed mixing with all the locals, who were justifiably excited about showing off their naval treasures. We were amazed to discover that back in the 15th century, the Venetian fleet had more than 300 ships and that in the 17th century, there had been 9,000 gondolas floating around the city. Nowadays, there are only about 400.

We ate delicious sarde in saor in a little bar opposite a white marble church.

Valerie and I crossed the Grand Canal on the No 2 Vaporetto over to the island of Giudecca. Originally called Spinalonga because of its fishbone-like shape, the island is full of beautiful churches and a long waterfront from where you can look across the lagoon to get a marvellous panoramic view of Venice city.

I have been lucky enough to visit Venice several more times over the years, sometimes with my friend Valerie and sometimes with my daughter and her best friend, Kemba.

During these visits, I explored so much more of this fascinating city, a city full of marvellous buildings and treasures. A city built centuries ago. A city built on water. A wonderful, beautiful, amazing place, full of character and history. A place I will never tire of visiting.

I stayed in different hotels and converted palaces along the Grand Canal. Once, we booked an Airbnb way off the beaten tourist path in a little neighbourhood full of local shops, hairdressers, and small family-run restaurants.

Every time I went I got lost, discovering areas of the city I had never been to before.

We visited La Fenice (Gran Teatro La Fenice), marvelling at the glorious, flamboyant architecture and decoration of the opera house. Despite suffering two devastating fires over the years, in 1836 and again in 1996, it has been rebuilt to its former glory and is a magnificent, wondrous place. It is a place of marble floors, sparkling chandeliers, and tiers of seating, its boxes richly decorated with frescos of cherubs and gilt.

Something I have found over the years is that Venice is often full of surprises.

One winter evening—I much prefer to visit the city in the colder months, rather than the height of summer when it is heaving with tourists—we came across a wonderful chocolate festival in a little square. We proceeded to thoroughly enjoy tasting the incredible artistic chocolate statues, bowls of fruit, and other such edible delights.

Another day during one of the trips, we crossed a bridge in the San Polo district and came across a bric-a-brac sale being held in a residential campo (square). I bought lots of cheap Murano glass souvenirs—damaged stock straight from the factories that were not good enough to be sold in the tourist shops.

As I was chatting to the lovely ladies behind the stall whilst my friend purchased some pretty earrings, a tall, handsome, and very charming Italian gentleman approached us. After talking with him for a bit, he invited me back to his apartment for lunch! The ladies, who turned out to know him very well, were extremely amused, and told me that although he was rather flirtatious, I would be very safe if I went with him. Appealing as the idea was, we were running short of time, so I graciously declined his kind offer. I often wonder how life would have turned out if I had accepted some of these random offers from gentlemen on my travels!

On every trip we visited a little shop near the Rialto Bridge, especially to buy some of their long liquorice sticks filled with different coloured candy.

I bought lots of handmade paper and beautiful leather-covered notebooks from ancient little shops that looked as though they had existed for several hundred years.

We ate far too much delicious gelato, but of course, that is a given!

One time, on a complete whim, I bought a little red metal tin jug from a small supermarket, and the friendly cashier explained that I should use it on a hot stove to boil my milk. I had only bought it as I liked the shape, so it was good to know it could actually serve a purpose!

Over the years I have bought far too many beautiful Italian bags on my journeys. They are made of the softest leather in every colour and style imaginable; there has been something new to tempt me every single time. Mostly I paid just 18 to 20 euros for each one, and as I still use them all to this day, they were definitely a good investment!

On my last visit back in 2019, my daughter, an art historian, took me to the Venice Biennale, which was a wonderful experience.

I always hate leaving Venice, fearful that I will never be lucky enough to return. Although I love whizzing across the lagoon in a fast motorboat, it makes me sad looking back as the city with all its towers, palaces, and bridges recedes into the distance.

I used to love the old airport right by the water's edge, but it has now been superseded by a sleek, modern, and efficient structure, better able to cope with the flood of tourists wanting to visit.

I must finish this Venice section by mentioning the benches.

On my first visit here in 2001, I was wandering 'round St. Mark's Square and asked my Italian friend, Manuela, whether all the benches stacked around the square were there for a festival or some kind of large gathering. She laughed, explaining that they were a necessity, there to cope with the Acqua Alta—the high water that invades the land when Venice gets flooded. The locals have to use the benches like a gangway to walk on, in order to get safely off the flooded streets!

AND THEN TO FLORENCE

I had never visited Florence, so when my art historian daughter suggested we should go there after Venice, I didn't hesitate. In those pre-Covid days, it was easy to plan impulse trips; there was absolutely no need to consider vaccination passports, scanning, or masks. How long ago that all seems now! After two years we have become rather used to the "new normal," where borders are closed, countries are on red lists, and we are all a little fearful of getting on a plane.

Back in 2018, however, this wasn't an issue. So, we happily made plans and booked hotels for our trip.

I had suggested that it would perhaps be fun to go from Venice to Florence on the train, rather than flying. If we did it this way, I thought we would be able to see all the beautiful Tuscan countryside without leaving the comfort of our seats. Well... how wrong I was!

I was excited as we boarded the train at Santa Lucia station. It was going to be such an exciting journey. Somehow, leaving Venice from the railway station was not as painful as my previous experiences of watching it disappear from the horizon as my boat sped across the lagoon to the airport.

There are many trains from Venice to Florence every day, so it was easy to get a reservation even in the height of the tourist season.

We had already tried out the train system a few days earlier when we went to Padua (Pàdova), a small city located 23 miles west of Venice.

This lovely ancient city was one of antiquity, churches, wonderful art, and a bustling university.

I particularly loved the Scrovegni Chapel, a wonderful little place with the most magnificent Giotto frescoes. They are frescoes on a bright blue background depicting the stories of the Virgin Mary and Christ in a unique way. They were completed in 1305. I would highly recommend a visit, but you will need to make reservations in advance! This treasure is very popular with both Italians and tourists alike.

But, back to the train journey.

It was going to take less than three hours to reach the Santa Maria Novella train station in Florence, but we had packed a few drinks and snacks for the journey, unsure of whether there was a restaurant on the train.

As it turned out, our snacks were the saving grace on this journey, as my much-trumpeted idea of seeing the Tuscan countryside from the comfort of our train seats did not really materialise. The high-speed train whizzed along, plunging into darkness far too often as we raced through long tunnels to reach our destination. Sadly, we probably would have seen more of the landscape if we had travelled by bus or plane instead. A good lesson learned!

Arriving in Florence, we were immediately stunned by the ancient beauty of the city, the capital of Tuscany and home to many masterpieces of art and architecture.

My daughter had planned and booked our itinerary down to the tiniest detail. From her home in London, she had made reservations for all the leading galleries and places of interest. Unfortunately, though they were intentionally planned this way, some of the bookings were incredibly early in the morning. We wanted to be able to study the treasures in relative peace before being surrounded by throngs of noisy tourists.

You could find us at the Uffizi Gallery before 8:00 am, or in the Galleria dell'Accademia, marvelling at Michelangelo's huge sculpture of David, before we had even had our breakfast! Then we would hurry back to our beautiful hotel, an ancient, restored palace near the Ponte Vecchio—the medieval stone bridge lined with jewellery shops. Once here, we sat on the beautiful terrace, overlooking the ancient city and enjoying fresh fruit, eggs, and the most delicious olive bread I have ever tasted.

There is truly so much to see in Florence. Like Venice, everywhere you look there are magnificent ancient buildings: churches, palaces, museums, and galleries. We wandered through the Piazza del Duomo and admired the Cathedral of Santa Maria del Fiore, the Baptistery, and Giotto's Campanile, all now part of the UNESCO World Heritage site that covers the historic centre of Florence.

On the recommendation of our hotel manager, we crossed the Ponte Santa Trinita (St. Trinity Bridge), the oldest elliptic bridge in the world, to dine at a local restaurant. Here, in a tiny room packed with locals and tourists, we dined on suckling pig.

It was something that none of us really fancied trying, but the charming elderly Italian man in the hotel assured us we would love it. And honestly, we did.

We left the restaurant—replete after many courses—and wandered to a nearby lively bar. Soon, we got into conversation with two young men from Dubai who were enjoying a final bachelor holiday before they flew home to settle down with an arranged marriage and children.

For me, quite apart from all the wonderful sights and sounds I see on my travels, meeting new people from different parts of the globe is one of my greatest joys.

Of course, along with turning strangers into friends, shopping is still another one of my greatest joys. Before leaving this fabulous city, I had to wander to the lovely leather market near the Ponte Vecchio. Here, I was persuaded to buy a rather beautiful red leather handbag and a bright yellow purse—both to remind me of my glorious stay!

COPENHAGEN

A weekend in Copenhagen sounded like a fabulous escape after the rather traumatic and turbulent time when my marriage fell apart.

Usually I prefer to organise my own travel plans, but I have realised that sometimes it can be left to others, just as long as they know you well.

Fortunately, my daughter Lucy knows me very well, so to cheer me up, she organised the most fabulous weekend.

I had never been to Denmark, so was quite excited when we arrived late in the evening in Copenhagen. We stayed in an Airbnb apartment in the centre of the city and I was amazed to see all the bikes lined up outside the smart apartment block. I had not realised it was such a popular form of transport there.

Lucy had been before, so she proved to be an excellent tour guide, ensuring I saw all the tourist sights that she knew would interest me. We saw Amalienborg Palace, the beautiful city gardens, the ancient cobbled streets, and the marvellous National Museum of Denmark, where we adored the *Danish Chair exhibition,* as both Lucy and I are rather passionate about chairs!

Such delights were interspersed with coffee and lunch stops in interesting places. We ate dinner in a cute restaurant that doubled up in the daytime as a bakery. They only served one set menu, but their popularity was such that people were happy to queue outside for ages until a table became available.

I embarrassed my daughter a little by staring for rather too long at several very attractive young Danish men. She was particularly mortified when I said that I was staring because they looked just like Vikings. My vivid imagination is always hovering!

We wandered the streets of the city for hours, and just as we were beginning to flag a little, we came across a very jolly event in a local square. Here, hundreds of locals were enjoying some sort of festival—a delight of beer, food, and music. We sat on the concrete, sipping our delicious beer and feeling very content in the Copenhagen sunshine!

On our last day, we caught a train out to the countryside to visit the Louisiana Museum of Modern Art, a marvellous place right by the seaside with gardens, sculptures, and a pleasant café!

Our weekend was over far too soon, but left so many happy memories.

LILLE, THE FLAMBOYANCE, AND THE TERROR

Lille had been on my bucket list for many years before I actually made it there.

It is a city in Northern France near the border of Belgium, once an important merchant centre of French Flanders.

The idea of this ancient city entranced me.

I had read of its rich history, from the Middle Ages to the French Revolution. Often besieged and occupied, it was a city that had known both great success as an industrial capital, and great destruction. Having been in decline for many years, it was reinvigorated in the late 1980s and 1990s with the arrival of the Eurostar train, an international airport, and a bustling university.

So, when I heard that the Gardening Club in our little English village was planning a day trip there, I booked my ticket.

We had to leave early to catch the ferry to France and then drive through the countryside to Lille. It promised to be a great day out.

Sadly, we never made it. The coach broke down on the French motorway and could not be fixed in time, so we had to spend the day in Calais instead. Now Calais is an attractive and interesting French seaside town, but I had been there several times before. Although we had fun, I was very disappointed at missing the opportunity to visit Lille.

Fast forward a few years and my friend Valerie was entertaining me with her description of a wonderful weekend she had just spent in Lille. Her talk of the great architecture, food, and fabulous markets made me rather green with envy, so we decided to book a trip there the following year.

That trip didn't pan out either; Valerie had an accident and we were forced to cancel our plans.

Finally, some years later, the stars aligned and the two of us made the trip. While only for a weekend, that would be plenty enough to see the sights and perhaps fit in a market or two!

We arrived at the main train station very late at night. It was dark and rather uninviting as we dragged our heavy cases over the cobbled streets, but fortunately our hotel was very nearby and we were glad to sink into our beds straightaway. We asked the hotel receptionist, a very charming young man, to book us an early wake-up call the next morning and a taxi to take us to a market that Valerie knew of on the outskirts of the town. He seemed most reluctant, saying that perhaps it wasn't advisable for us to visit such an insalubrious part of town. Valerie assured him we would be fine, and insisted he book our taxi.

The next day even the taxi driver seemed concerned; apparently we (at the ages of 60- and 70-something) were considered far too old for such adventures!

We seemed to drive around for ages, and as he slowed down near the approach to the market, I was beginning to wonder if perhaps this visit was so wise after all. The streets were rather grubby—unlike the pristine historic centre of town where we were staying—and there was graffiti everywhere. Even written in French, it seemed a little threatening. But hey, we were women of the world! It was a bright, sunny morning. What could possibly go wrong?

Walking into the entrance of the open market we were instantly reassured. Everywhere we looked there were the usual stalls found in a traditional French street market: flowers, bread and cheese, patterned tablecloths, linen dresses, and artisan soaps. There were loads of fresh fruit and vegetables. All was well, and in no time our arms were full of woven baskets stuffed to the brim with such treasures.

Then we turned a corner and everything changed. The country stalls, filled with their fresh produce, gave way to stall after stall of burqas, the full-length outfits that covered the entire body with a mesh screen covering the eyes. Although we knew they were worn by some traditional Islamic women throughout the world, we had not expected to encounter these for sale in a French market. There were almost no women around, just men behind the stalls, stalls which also stocked small burqas, apparently to be worn by little girls. The contrast was so vast that we were a bit shocked, especially as we no longer saw women milling about once we went into that part of the space. After leaving the market, we decided to get a taxi back to the city.

Unfortunately, being in a residential area, taxis were not plentiful, so after a while we decided to take the train instead. Walking through the streets of this rather rundown neighbourhood while struggling with all our shopping made it so that we were delighted to finally reach the station. Fortunately, even with our little amount of French speaking abilities, we managed to get on the right train and find our way back to the hotel. The receptionist from the night before at the Hôtel Lille Europe—the rather attractive young Black man—was delighted to see us return safely.

"*Oh Mesdames, we have been so worried about you. That is not a good area for you to have travelled to alone. But you are safely back with us now. I suggest you go and have a nice lunch to recover!*"

And so we took his advice.

We wandered to the historic centre, marvelling at all the magnificent buildings en route. Cobbled streets lined with 17th century brick townhouses—houses that had seen so much history. We ate a delicious lunch outside a little restaurant in General de Gaulle Square and drank plenty of wine. Then we wandered the city, stopping to admire some of the ancient buildings and shops in the maze of narrow streets. We visited the Old Stock Exchange building (La Vieille Bourse), a historical monument and splendid example of 17th century Flemish Renaissance style. There was a second-hand book market there, and I purchased a rather beautiful hand-made antique book to take home for my daughter.

Exhausted by all our adventures, we decided to have a light dinner and retire to bed early.

However, this trip was full of surprises, and even that idea didn't go to plan!

While walking back to the hotel, we noticed lots of decorations in the main square. Upon enquiring with our receptionist friend, we discovered that a Mardi Gras procession was taking place that night. We decided to watch it from the first floor restaurant area, a room with floor to ceiling windows that would give us a bird's-eye view.

We watched as all the performers assembled in the car park opposite. The floats and costumes were spectacular. It was all so colourful and exciting. But of course, we were on the inside, looking out.

"*Why don't we just pop outside, so we feel part of it?*"

We both agreed it would be fun. We would only go for a few minutes, then straight back to bed. We didn't even need to go up to the room to get our bags; we wouldn't need our money or phones, we were only going to stand outside the hotel.

Somehow though (and not surprisingly), we got caught up in the festive atmosphere. I had never been to Rio or New Orleans, but had always wanted to visit both. This seemed like a good second-best for now! Within ten minutes, we decided to "*just follow the procession down to the main square,*" only five minutes or so away from the hotel.

The feel of the environment was wonderful. The colours, the excitement, the performers, the music, the admiring crowds. We followed the beautiful chaos towards the square, soaking up the carnival atmosphere and loving every moment.

But then, it started to go wrong. Suddenly, hundreds of people were all trying to get through the narrow streets at the same time. Everybody started jostling for space. It was a hot evening and all of a sudden, people found themselves squashed together in a small space, rather like sardines in a can. A young mother pushing a pram started screaming that her children were being crushed. Everyone panicked, grinding to a halt trying to help her, but then more people came onto the little street and it became a true nightmare. People were pushing each other, women were screaming, and I felt myself being hemmed in by lots of hot, sweaty bodies. Valerie and I were wedged together in a raging mass of humanity. Then, I heard her cry out and turned 'round to see her being lifted above the crowd by a giant of a man, who placed her carefully and safely on a nearby window ledge. She held out her hand, calling to me as I was swept past. It was one of the worst moments of my life. I understand now how people get crushed in panic. Just a few minutes before, everyone had been happy and laughing, enjoying the spectacle of the Mardis Gras; now those same people were fighting for their freedom, each one seemingly pitted against the other.

Almost as soon as it started, it was over. The heaving crowd suddenly turned into the main square and all the people dispersed. It was as if the bottle in which we had all been trapped had suddenly popped open, ejecting us all at speed.

I was very shaken, but after a few minutes, I had calmed down enough to enjoy the concert that was taking place. There were jugglers, fire dancers, and acrobats. The vibrant and colourful carnival was now in full swing. But where was Valerie? Surely she would get down off that ledge and come join me soon?

I waited another 15 minutes before I ventured back to look for her. A few people were still arriving, but nothing like the crowd we had experienced. I wandered up and down the little lane, searching for her in vain. There was no way I could have missed her; there was only one entrance onto the square.

Using my very basic French, I asked a few people if they had seen her. Surely someone must have noticed an elderly lady standing on a window ledge?

I waited in that square until the show was over, convinced that she would turn up eventually. As the crowds started to disperse, I realised I would have to give up. She had obviously returned to the hotel without me.

I retraced my steps to go back the way we had come, but unfortunately the gendarmes (police) had closed off the street. That forced the crowds to take a different route. I had no choice but to follow them blindly. Lille was only quite small—it would be easy enough to get my bearings and find my way home.

Soon, the crowds began to thin out. There weren't so many people to follow, just a few family groups who obviously knew exactly where they were going. We came to a park, but I knew that was the wrong way, so I turned right and was relieved to see a group of gendarmes ahead. I went up to them and tried to explain my predicament: that I was alone and lost, that my elderly friend and I were separated in the crowd, and that I was worried about her. They barely listened, obviously thought I was just a mad (or drunk) English tourist, and pointed me in the opposite direction muttering something that sounded like, *"just head for the main road."*

By now I was beginning to get a bit worried for myself too. It was dark, I was in a strange city, wandering around alone with no sense of direction and no money or phone. I wasn't even certain as to exactly where our hotel was, I just knew it was near the train station.

The time ticked by. It was getting pretty late. The bars and restaurants were all beginning to close up for the night and I now found myself in a rather seedy-looking part of town. It was probably perfectly fine in the daylight, but somehow when you are alone and scared, everything seems like a danger. The two young men smoking outside the apartment building. The man in leather standing by his motorbike. There were very few people around. I was beginning to panic, to think that I would never see Valerie, my hotel, or my precious daughter in England again.

And then I met my guardian angel.

By now it was eleven o'clock at night; I had been wandering aimlessly for more than an hour and there was hardly a soul in sight. I was getting cold and limping quite badly, having recently recovered from a knee operation.

I saw two elderly ladies chatting on a street corner, their little dogs beside them. Almost in tears, I went up to them and asked for directions to the railway station. My French is poor at the best of times and neither lady spoke English, but the younger of the two took pity on me, gave her little dog to her friend to take home, and said she would escort me to where I needed to go herself.

Never in my whole life have I been so grateful to another human being. Without her help, I am not sure what would have happened. I was getting more and more anxious, almost to the end of my tether, but after a few minutes in her company I had calmed down, confident that she would indeed get me back safely.

Somehow we managed to converse, she seemed to understand my broken French and certainly understood my gratitude—my constant mutterings of "*merci beaucoup, je suis perdue.*"

After walking for about 15 minutes in quite the opposite direction to the one I had been heading, we reached the station, and in the distance I could see the lights of my hotel. I don't think I have ever felt such utter relief in all my life.

I thanked her profusely, hugging her in gratitude, but before she allowed me to go, she dragged me into the station forecourt and pointed to the ceiling.

She wanted me to see the new sculptures, recently installed. I looked up to see several giant white clouds with figures, including an angel with wings, sitting atop them. Somehow, it seemed incredibly fitting.

We hugged goodbye and she watched until I reached the safety of my hotel. I turned to wave a final thank you just as Valerie and the hotel receptionist came rushing out. They both hugged me, delighted I had returned in one piece. Apparently, after our ordeal and once the crowd had dispersed, Valerie waited a little while for me to come back, then assumed I had already gone back to the hotel. She returned there herself and then waited anxiously for hours, assuming something dreadful had happened to me.

So, the moral of this story is: Never go out without your money, phone, a map, and an idea of where you live!

Lille, in the end, you were quite an experience.

CHINA

My daughter Lucy phoned me from London, one grey and damp February day in 2017. It was a sunny summer day here in New Zealand, and I had just come in from relaxing in the garden.

"Mum, you've always wanted to go to China, haven't you? Why don't we go together?"

I needed no persuading, so two months later I boarded a plane in Auckland, headed for Shanghai.

She was flying from London and we had arranged to meet at a hotel in Beijing.

Another adventure.

Although we were both pretty experienced travellers by now, neither of us had been to China before and we didn't speak Mandarin, so it seemed sensible to seek a bit of help booking some aspects of the trip. There was a lot on our agenda and we didn't want to waste time, so I booked English speaking drivers for the days we wanted to visit certain places. That proved to be a very wise decision, as without them I think we would have struggled a bit.

The first day we planned to see the Forbidden City and the Summer Palace, but when we got there it was heaving with local people enjoying a public holiday. The queues at the ticket offices were enormous, however, our lovely guide, Vincent, managed to bypass these and emerge after just ten minutes or so brandishing tickets—our passports to these wonderful sights.

I wanted to cry as I stood in Tiananmen Square (which, incidentally, was enormous, much larger than I had imagined). I had dreamt for so long of visiting this fascinating country and here I was, just a stone's throw away from stepping inside the Forbidden City, a place where only Emperors, their concubines, and eunuchs had lived for centuries. Behind the vast stone walls lay so many treasures, so many old secrets.

If you have seen the movie "*The Last Emperor,*" the place will seem very familiar to you, although I found it to be a much larger complex than I ever imagined, truly a city within a city. Afterwards, we travelled to the Summer Palace, another place of great majesty, and here we took a boat ride out on the lake. We enjoyed sharing this trip with local families, scarcely another tourist in sight.

After the first day, I was hooked. Already, I was in love with China.

We were so lucky to have such a fabulous guide. He was incredibly intelligent and entertained us with tales of the ancient places we were visiting, but also stories of his time working as a guide at the Beijing Olympics in 2008.

The next day we drove out to the Great Wall of China. Again there were huge crowds of locals at the ticket machines as it was still a public holiday, but once we were actually on the wall itself, the crowds thinned out and for much of the time we were almost alone, the three of us marvelling at the ancient construction built so long ago amongst an impressive backdrop. We climbed the well-worn steps, staring in amazement as the wall continued its path, snaking through the countryside for many miles. Truly, it is one of the world's great treasures.

On the way home we stopped at a delightful little restaurant, tucked in the countryside beneath the wall, and had the most delicious lunch with fresh watermelon as dessert. We soon realised that watermelon would always be served in preference to any other sweet treat, as apparently it is excellent for your digestion. We drank jasmine tea, as we were to do for almost the entire trip. In fact, I think we only had wine once during our entire visit to China, during our stay at a rather smart hotel in Xi'an.

We visited a silk factory where we watched, fascinated, as all the little silkworms performed their duties. Then we bought silk duvets and pillowcases, which the factory cleverly vacuum-packed to be ready to fit into our suitcases. We also indulged in a few pairs of beautiful silk pyjamas, and dressing gowns emblazoned with traditional Chinese good luck symbols.

Once we had seen these main sights, we spent the next couple of days alone, with no guide, just exploring the city for ourselves. We visited tiny, off-the-beaten-path markets and small shops. Lucy had done lots of research, so we also visited art galleries in converted factories and old, derelict buildings.

After our time in Beijing, we caught the bullet train to Xi'an. We were sad to say goodbye to Vincent; he had become a friend throughout our stay. He carefully deposited us at the first-class lounge in the station, ensuring that we knew exactly what time and which platform from which our train left. As he bowed a polite goodbye, we could tell that he was a little worried about us hurtling around the country—two women alone without the protection of a man.

I had booked us first-class tickets on the bullet train, as they were not too expensive and seemed to offer a degree more comfort than either the second- or third-class option.

I was so glad to have gotten the explicit instructions about how to board the train. It seemed as though half the population of the city was also on our train to Xi'an. Although the crowds jostled each other, they were very respectful of us, two European women struggling with our heavy luggage and unsure of which part of the train we were supposed to be heading to.

It all changed as we boarded. We were greeted by two smiling young women in smart uniforms who escorted us through the sliding doors to the first-class carriage. They settled us into our comfortable reclining seats and brought us cups of hot jasmine tea.

For the vast majority of that six-hour-long journey, we were the only passengers in the luxurious carriage. We were given comfortable slippers, silk eye masks and blankets, and throughout the trip, the lovely ladies kept appearing with snacks, meals, and drinks. Most of these things were unrecognisable to us; we could not read the Chinese labels and the women did not speak any English!

Overall, it was a fascinating ride and I stayed awake the whole time, gazing out of the window as we sped through the countryside. It was nothing like I had imagined. We saw vast panoramas of countryside, with traditional red-roofed villages and farms in the foreground and huge skyscraper buildings behind them. In the distance, there were huge factory buildings with smoke billowing across the skyline. Mile after mile of the same. Town after town full of industry. So much pollution.

Then there were large, brand new roads, multi-lane highways with absolutely no traffic. Although apparently during rush hour—when the factories open in the morning and close at night—the roads get clogged with worker's cars.

We stopped at various stations for people to disembark along the way. At one stop I was very amused to see two men get off the train, light up cigarettes, and then stand directly under a huge sign that said "NO SMOKING." It was written in Mandarin, but the big cigarette with the red line through it was a dead giveaway!

Eventually, we reached Xi'an. It was another bustling city with a frantically busy train station, so I was glad we had booked a driver and guide to pick us up and take us to our hotel.

"*My name is Linda, and this is our driver.*" She pointed to the middle-aged lady by her side, who smiled shyly at us. Despite me asking, we were not told her name. She never spoke to us, and for the duration of our stay we merely smiled at each other.

"*You have been assigned to us because we are also women. It is not fitting for you ladies to have male guides and drivers.*"

I did not mention that we had been very happy with our male guide and driver in Beijing.

As we drove through the bustling city, she pointed out all the sights.

"Of course that is only a five-star hotel, not as good as yours. You are the first six-star guests I have ever had."

She repeated this at every smart hotel we passed. Lucy and I smiled at each other, certain that we were just misunderstanding her words.

As we pulled up outside our hotel I was surprised to see two doormen in top hats and tails come to open our car doors. The hotel, from the exterior, was not aesthetically appealing. It was a huge concrete construction, built during the Cultural Revolution to house important party members and visiting dignitaries. Inside however, it was unbelievably luxurious. There were huge glittering chandeliers and shiny marble floors. Linda insisted on joining us as we got checked in, sitting on soft velvet couches, sipping more jasmine tea, and being attended by a beautiful young receptionist wearing a smart black dinner suit. By the time we reached our room I was getting anxious. Had I misread the information on the website? Maybe I had missed a few noughts from the price? Surely all this luxury couldn't be had for the price we paid?

But, everything was all right. After scrutinising the prices in the room brochure, I began to relax. In fact, I was so relaxed that I allowed Lucy to send a few items to the hotel laundry. They came back exquisitely pressed and presented in a beautiful box. Unfortunately, the cost of that service was almost the same as a decent dinner for two with wine, so we decided not to repeat the process!

The next morning, Linda and the lady driver arrived early to take us to see the Terracotta Warriors. We had arranged to meet them outside the hotel at 8:00 am, so we were surprised to see them an hour earlier while on our way to breakfast, lounging in the velvet armchairs in the hotel lobby. Apparently they just wanted to experience some of the luxury for themselves!

I absolutely loved our visit to see the warriors, they were a sight so wonderful that it made me cry. I had read all about them, but somehow, seeing them in that immense building—so many more than I had imagined—made me very emotional.

Our few days in Xi'an passed in a flurry.

We spent the rest of the time alone, exploring the city. We visited shops and markets, buying rice paper paintings, embroidered cushions, silk pyjamas, Mahjong sets, and teapots. I even bought a replica of a Terracotta Warrior from a small factory; they promised to ship it back to New Zealand for me.

We thoroughly enjoyed back street food stalls and the experience of the markets, although we found the sight of row upon row of roasted baby ducks and fried seahorses rather distressing.

Wandering around these markets, I suddenly remembered another trip. It was probably the one that sparked my interest in China. I was about nine or ten years old and we had a rare family outing, a trip to London to see the Christmas lights. I can still remember the excitement I felt as we walked around the city, the bright lights of the Christmas decorations in Oxford and Regent Street, the architecture, cobbled streets, and little alleyways. As we walked through Soho, Mum pointed out all the places she had known from her days working as a young apprentice tailor.

I had never seen her so animated.

I guess being stuck at home in the country for years with three small children, no family support, and not much money, dampens your enthusiasm for life a bit, so I was thrilled to see her so happy.

Then we wandered into Chinatown, a place I had never been until that point.

Back in the late 1950s, a time much less sophisticated than these days, Chinatown seemed so exciting to a little girl with a big imagination like me. Many of the shopkeepers still wore their traditional dress and the shop and restaurant windows were full of exotic foods and trinkets.

My dad bought Mum a gift, a little ornament of a rickshaw carrying a rather elegant lady in traditional dress with bound feet. It is only small, no more than four inches long and made of plastic I think, but it resembled bone and was very detailed. There was jade-coloured painting on the lady's dress and the coolie's jacket, as well as on the scenery painted on the back of the rickshaw. It probably only cost a few pounds, but it became a family treasure, locked away in the china cabinet and only to be viewed through the glass. It now sits on my desk, next to a photo of my beloved, deceased parents, and I look at it often and smile, remembering that happy day.

Imagine therefore, the thrill I felt when I saw an almost identical one at the Museum of Qin Terracotta Warriors and Horses, although it was a bit larger and made of rather more valuable material!

I really do believe this is why things bought on your travels are so important, not for their intrinsic value, but for the memories they hold—memories that can last a lifetime.

On our last morning in Xi'an, Linda and the lady driver arrived early to collect us. Our luggage had already been taken downstairs, so Lucy and I descended the grand staircase with just our hand luggage.

"But where is all your shopping? I left you alone for two days to shop!"

Linda momentarily stopped yelling instructions to our driver and the two porters, who were attempting to load all our luggage into the rather small car boot.

Her face dropped when I said that we had managed to squeeze it all into our three large suitcases.

"But you went shopping—where are all your bags? Your Gucci and Prada bags?"

Poor Linda. She was so disappointed when I told her that all our shopping had come from cheap, but fascinating, little back street shops and markets. She was crestfallen.

"But you are my first ever six-star guests. I was telling all my friends about you."

She was very quiet on the way back to the train station. We had obviously really let her down.

We caught the bullet train to Shanghai and again, I was fascinated as we whizzed through the countryside at speed. It was almost exactly the same as the previous journey—old traditional villages, which must have been there for centuries, were gradually being squeezed out by huge factories billowing obnoxious smoke all over their hard-tended crops and farms. There were blocks after blocks of huge apartment buildings, some derelict, some brand new, all obviously built to accommodate the millions of workers for the factories.

It made me a bit sad. The old China I had read about in the Look and Learn magazines was long gone. The traditional way of life was now only found in museums, books, or murals painted on walls. China was now in the forefront of the modern world, every shopping mall was stuffed full of electronic gadgets and mobile phones galore.

Talking of mobile phones, we visited an old village just outside of Shanghai known as the Venice of Shanghai. Here we went on a little boat on the lagoon and admired all the old shop houses lining the banks. We ate lunch at a lovely traditional restaurant, a place of dark corners, red lanterns, and old wooden chairs. Our guide, Miranda, a beautiful young Chinese woman much the same age as Lucy, insisted that we try the local pork delicacy. As we did not understand anything written on the menu, we agreed to everything she suggested. When the food was delivered and placed on a revolving dish in the middle of our table, she dispensed advice as to what we should try first. It was all quite delicious, even the local pork dish. Suddenly I realised that she was avoiding the pork dish altogether.

"*Miranda, why aren't you eating that one? You recommended it so highly.*"

She laughed.

"*Oh no, I hate that, I never eat it. It's horrible. But as tourists, you should try everything.*"

After lunch we strolled around the ancient village, admiring the little houses and bridges that had been so well restored. I stopped to take a photograph of the bucolic scene; as I checked the image on my phone, I realised that all the locals—both young and old—in the picture were busy looking at their phones, not taking in the beauty of the place at all. Such is the modern world!

Later, strolling along the famous Bund whilst I was soaking up all the sights, the old colonial buildings nestled alongside towering shiny new edifices, Lucy and Miranda were deep in conversation about how hard it was for young, educated women such as themselves to find a decent life partner. It seemed that nowadays, young men the world over were often unwilling to commit to one girl, preferring instead to sow their wild oats!

We visited the old Colonial quarter, went to art galleries, and I dragged Lucy into an enormous four-storey stationery shop. There, I bought notebooks, pens, fancy erasers, and rulers.

Our trip to China was over far too soon, but there are so many other highlights of the visit that are etched into my memory.

The kindness of the locals.

Finding some of our rather expensive French luggage at a much-reduced price in a little back street mall in Xi'an.

Chatting to an old, wrinkled lady at her little market stall about her beautiful embroidered cushions. It seemed that her mother had worked for a European family back in the 1940s and they had sent her to school so she could learn English. Apparently, she had been one of the only girls in her class.

Laughing with sales ladies in little back street shops when we realised that even their XXL-sized garments were still too tiny for my European body!

Talking to the owner of a furniture shop that sold the most exquisite hand-painted lacquer pieces. He told me that "*nowadays, only middle-aged people buy this stuff—the young ones much prefer Ikea.*"

Standing in a remote warehouse, rather like an old aircraft hangar, gazing up in awe at the giant artworks of KAWS. The Mickey Mouse-type figures were huge and imposing against the stark concrete and steel background of the old, rather derelict building.

China more than matched up to my childhood dreams, and one day I hope to go again! I'd love to make more memories in this fascinating country.

ANNUAL TRIPS BACK TO LONDON

It is very strange how you can spend the first 59 years of your life living in one place, and then one day feel that somehow you don't belong there anymore.

Having spoken to many immigrants over the years, people from all kinds of places, this seems to be something many of us have in common. Somehow, once you have made the decision to emigrate, you don't really feel that you actually belong anywhere. Most of us love our new adopted countries, but somehow we still feel a bit like outsiders too.

Sadly, I now feel a bit like that about England.

I will always love Britain and be proud of my heritage, but somehow it doesn't seem like my country anymore. Every time I go back I am happy to visit, delighted to catch up with the friends and family I have missed so badly and eager to soak up the best parts of my homeland.

I long for the beautiful countryside, winding country lanes, the shops, the ancient towns and cities, village pubs, bluebell woods, the stuff I have known all my life. And yet,

I often feel like I do not belong. This is the price you pay for wanting a different life, a life less ordinary.

Until COVID hit, I was lucky enough to go back every year. It was a trip I looked forward to passionately, a way of retaining my links to the old country without having to give up any of my glorious new life on the other side of the world.

A FIJIAN FUNERAL

Since living there in the 1970s, Fiji always held a very special place in my heart. I looked forward so much to every visit and always felt completely at home as soon as I stepped off the plane onto Fijian soil.

Of course, having a loving extended family to come back to made every visit worthwhile. There were always new babies, new cousins, aunties, and uncles to meet, but at the heart of it all was my beloved Naomi.

Naomi, the wonderful woman who started out as my housekeeper and became one of my absolutely most-cherished friends. We were so different, two women from different cultures who led totally different lives, yet we had a true bond. It was somehow stronger than the bond between blood sisters, one made of mutual love, respect, and understanding for one another. This bond lasted 42 years, despite us spending most of that time apart, on opposite ends of the world.

When I stepped off the plane in Fiji in 2018, I could hardly wait for the next day to arrive so that I could go and visit Naomi as planned. I looked forward to another day of joy and laughter with my friend.

Sadly, that was not to be. I got a call early the next morning that my beloved Naomi had passed away, unexpectedly and far too soon. We had only just celebrated her 75th birthday a few months earlier. I was bereft. I would never see her beautiful face again.

Everyone who has loved deeply will know the depth of my sorrow. I was absolutely beside myself, heartbroken.

Her funeral will live forever in my heart.

The Fijian way of grieving is much healthier than ours. People do not try to keep a stiff upper lip, instead, they allow their grief and sorrow to show. Therefore, it seemed quite natural for me to prostrate myself across Naomi's coffin, weeping loudly and not caring what others might have thought.

I wept as I said a few words about my best friend at the church service and wept again as they lowered her body into the ground, covering her coffin with beautiful traditional tapa cloth. I felt honoured that I was allowed to take part in such a personal family affair.

Another chapter in my life was over, but the friendship between Naomi and me will always be known and remembered. I was happy that there were now threads for the next generation to weave; my Lucy already held my Fijian family in her heart and I knew they felt the same about her.

MOROCCO

"M*um, why don't we go to Morocco? I know you'll love it.*"

Once again, my daughter was right. She knows me so well. She knows and understands my wanderlust, my desire to explore the world, to discover new places. It is not just about the typical tourist destinations, but also about places that are a little different, places where I could get to know the locals a little and spark my imagination.

I had been visiting Lucy in London, so we flew from Stansted Airport to Marrakesh. As I walked through the terminal building I felt the same sense of excitement that I had experienced when I visited Tunisia and Egypt, even though these were different North African countries with their own unique cultures and identities.

This time there were three of us travelling—Lucy, her best friend Kemba, and me. Three single women, two of whom were beautiful single girls in their twenties. This ensured that for the whole trip, we had excellent attention from most of the men we met—nothing was too much trouble for them. There is no doubt that lovely young women who are interested and empathetic to the world around them, attract good vibes.

Rather than staying in Marrakesh itself, we had opted to drive straight to Essaouira, a port and seaside town on the Atlantic coast. We would come back to Marrakesh for the last couple of nights of our stay.

Essaouira. I even find myself smiling as I type the name. I had not expected to be so enchanted by the place.

"An exceptional example of a late 18th century fortified town. Known for a long time as the Port of Timbuktu, it became one of the major Atlantic commercial centres between Africa and Europe in the 18th and 19th centuries."

The girls had booked our stay at the Villa Maroc hotel, the same place they had stayed and loved on their last visit. Soon after arriving I could quite see why. Nestled in the ancient medina, it was a calm, cool, and relaxing escape from the heat outside.

From the moment we stepped outside the hotel into the narrow streets of the medina, I was completely hooked. Unlike some souks I had visited throughout the world, there was a calmness here. It might have been because it was slightly out of the main tourist season, or because we had arrived during the festival of Ramadan, but it was a joy to wander the streets without being hassled to buy something at every turn. On that first afternoon alone, without any encouragement, I bought beautiful scarves, woven baskets, colourful pottery tagines, and fossils. I must mention the fossils in more detail.

Dallying a little behind the girls who walked much faster than I did, I came across a fascinating little shop piled high, floor to ceiling, with treasures. There were many different things: old lamps, statues, and fabrics, but the pieces that caught my eye were the ammonites and fossils—piles and piles of fossils. Some were small, only a few inches in diameter, but others were enormous and incredibly heavy. Some were polished, but most were in their natural state.

I chatted to the elderly gentleman sitting on the floor; apparently the little shop had belonged to his now-deceased father who had collected the fossils over many years. I was pretty desperate to buy some, particularly the largest and heaviest of them all, but realised I would never be able to get them home to New Zealand as they would far exceed my travel allowance weight.

Instead, I contented myself by purchasing just a few, knowing I would still treasure them however small they were. I had already decided that I would return to this fascinating city one day, so I could work out a way of buying and transporting something larger next time.

The three of us were rather weary by this point, so as we were passing a little tea shop where a charming gentleman invited us in to try his "special teas," we followed him inside to rest a while. This turned out to be one of the best decisions we could have made.

Hichame, the charming gentleman who had offered us tea, turned out to be a well-educated intelligent man who could speak not just Arabic and French, but also English and Italian. While he was pouring our tea in that incredibly dramatic way that we came to know so well, he told us a little of his life and the life of Essaouira.

He told us stories of the ancient port, now a thriving fishing village packed with small blue boats. It was previously better known as a thriving industrial and slave trading port. He said that was a dark and shameful part of their history—a part which most people would rather forget.

He offered to take us on a little walking tour of the medina after I had expressed a desire to buy some cheap silver jewellery. As we walked 'round the winding alleyways, he pointed out buildings of interest and told us a little more of the city's history. Rather than letting me buy my jewellery from one of the little shops we passed, "*far too expensive, they will overcharge you,*" he led us to a little back alley, a quiet place frequented only by locals.

He knocked on the door of a tiny shop and it was opened by a handsome Bedouin man in white robes. I was entranced. I had never met a proper Bedouin man before. He explained to us that, although he usually led a nomadic existence in the desert, he would always come into town for the period of Ramadan to sell the exquisite jewellery his tribe had made. Although they largely still lived in the traditional way by bartering, apparently the demands of the modern world meant that they now also needed to have regular supplies of cash to purchase some of life's necessities—like mobile phones!

The jewellery they had made was fascinating, designed for the local market rather than the tourist one. Many of the pieces were large and very flamboyant. The entire shop was packed with silver trinkets of every imaginable kind. It took ages for me to make my selections—there was so much to choose from—but in the end I settled on a necklace. It was a very unusual piece with a small silver and black replica of the tool they use in the desert to find their way, a very attractive kind of compass. I also chose a ring with an unusual red and turquoise pattern, and a very beautiful wide silver bracelet. The man was delighted that I selected this particular piece and remarked on my good taste; apparently it was an antique Berber piece (on later investigation, this proved to be absolutely true). The bracelet was a little big for me, so he adjusted it right there and then. I still felt it could be a bit tighter, but his response rather took my breath away. "*Once you are my wife living in a tent in the desert, you will need it that loose so that you can push it up your arm to keep it safe while you are doing the washing up*." Obviously, despite his rather flirtatious manner, and the fact that he was young enough to be my son, he had no intention of making me a senior wife who lazed around eating dates. Rather, he assumed I would fill a position a bit lower down the ranks, perhaps wife number five or six. We all laughed as I solemnly advised him that, perhaps under those circumstances, I could not marry him after all. It was a very happy encounter, one that still makes me smile when I think about it. Perhaps one day we can accept his kind invitation to visit his tribe and see how modern day Bedouins live.

Our new friend Hichame, from the tea shop, was a Berber from a village below the Atlas Mountains. We visited his tea shop again the next day and this time, he took us through the medina to meet the ladies at an argan oil cooperative. That was another lovely meeting that culminated in lasting friendship and an invitation to visit the women's home in the mountains. One day, we will.

In the late afternoon we wandered down to the harbour, fascinated to watch the fisherman selling their catch while small boys and young men dived into the water and hungry birds circled overhead.

Essaouira is apparently the third-most important sardine fishing port in Morocco, although sole, bream, swordfish, and sharks (which make excellent fish tagine) are also caught there.

From the fishing port you can see the ramparts from the old medina walls. They are very impressive, built hundreds of years ago to withstand invasion. In fact, they are so impressive that they were used as a backdrop for the popular Game of Thrones series.

Our stay in this delightful city was too short. We made time to wander on the beach, eat delicious food, and enjoy glorious breakfasts on the sunny rooftop of our little hotel that overlooked the ocean. However, there was so much we didn't have time to do, so it is certainly on our bucket lists to return.

We spent the last couple of nights of our trip back in Marrakesh. It was a fun time and we stayed in a lovely little riad, a calming, atmospheric place that made you forget that the bustling noisy lanes of the medina were just outside your door. I absolutely loved the souks and managed to buy even more to squeeze into my already overflowing luggage: a traditional-style silver tea set so I could practice the elaborate tea pouring that Hichame had taught us, more scarves and linen trousers, and another handbag.

We wandered through quiet green gardens and sat and drank glasses of mint tea. It was a calm oasis within the bustling city.

I enjoyed our time in Marrakesh, but my heart was back in Essaouira. That was my new favourite city in Africa.

BACK TO THE ARMCHAIR, BUT STILL DREAMING!

Due to the ongoing Covid-19 pandemic, my plans, like those of the rest of the world's travellers, have been put on hold. However, there is still so much left on my bucket list.

I realise I have left some memories out. This was not done intentionally, but that's the funny thing about memories. They pop back into your mind just when you least expect them.

So here are a few extra memories, in no particular order of importance.

Amsterdam: tulip fields, bicycles, shops full of hundreds of brightly-coloured wooden clogs, blue and white Delft pottery, the Red Light District, canals, and windmills.

Sydney: The Rocks, getting a bus to Bondi Beach, catching a ferry to Manly, visiting friends in Cronulla and Caringbah, harbour cruises, wonderful firework displays, big yellow ducks floating in Darling Harbour, a trip to the Blue Mountains only to find them shrouded in mist, and the Hyde Park Barracks (now a wonderful museum where you can learn all about the life of early convicts—sad and haunting stories that were buried for years).

Terraces of pretty little houses with wrought-iron balconies, sad-eyed Aboriginal Australians playing their didgeridoos for tourists at Circular Quay, the Sydney Opera House, Sydney Harbour Bridge, and the Queen Victoria Building.

A fabulous winery north of Melbourne, where we wandered up to the edge of the vineyard at sunset to see families of wild kangaroos.

I could go on forever.

I am surrounded by so many memories of my *Seventy Years' Worth of Travels.*

A Terracotta Warrior, an Egyptian pharaoh, shells, rocks, books, and stationery galore. I have hand blown misshapen paperweights, fossils, Mahjong sets, black handmade pottery, leather handbags, rice paper paintings, and tapa cloth. The list is endless. Somehow, looking at these things just makes me more restless, because I realise there is still so much of the world that needs to be explored.

Pre-lockdown, I had booked a trip to Russia, Helsinki, Tallinn, and Riga, so hopefully one day I will get to those places. On my bucket list there is also New Orleans, Texas, South Carolina, and much more of the USA and Canada, lots more of Europe, Australia, and even more of my home base of New Zealand.

Every time I watch a travel show or read a holiday review, something else gets added to my list, so I am definitely going to have to live to at least a hundred years old to stand a chance of seeing everything.

THE END

AUTHOR BIOGRAPHY

Pat Backley is an English woman who, at the age of 59, decided to become a Kiwi.

She now lives in New Zealand. When not writing, Pat loves to travel the world and catch up with all her friends (COVID permitting). She particularly enjoys spending lots of time in Fiji with her beloved extended Fijian family.

She also gardens, paints, reads, and loves activities like interior design, walks on the beach, and socialising. In short, she lives an ideal existence, but it wasn't always this easy. You can learn more about Pat's life by reading her recently published memoirs: *FROM THERE TO HERE, WITH AN AWFUL LOT IN BETWEEN.*

This book:

SEVENTY YEARS' WORTH OF TRAVEL: SNIPPETS FROM A COLOURFUL AND INTERESTING LIFE (published 2022)

Pat's other publications include two books in the DAISY historical saga series: *DAISY* (published 2020) and *THE SECOND DAISY* (published 2021).

The first book in her new ANCESTORS series: *VALENTINE GEORGE,* was published in early 2022.

In 2021 she also co-authored a coffee table book:

THE WARRIOR WOMEN PROJECT: A SISTERHOOD OF IMMIGRANT WOMEN.

www.ingramcontent.com/pod-product-compliance
Lightning Source LLC
Chambersburg PA
CBHW021157110726
47900CB00002B/620